CONUS Battle Drills

A Guide for Combat Veterans to Corporate Life, Parenthood, and Caging the Beast Inside

By

Louis Jonathan Fernandez

CONUS Battle Drills

ISBN-13: 978-1522903352

ISBN-10: 1522903356

Contents

Introduction

Every day thousands of combat veterans enter the civilian world. They are either retiring, or fulfilling an obligation and now they need to navigate a world that they are completely unprepared for. What do I want to do with my life? Where do I want to live? How do I find a job? I have to provide for my family, am I prepared to make this leap? It is a very stressful time, and most of us are figuring it out on the fly. What if you had a guide that could tell you exactly what to expect, what pitfalls to avoid, tips and tricks for surviving in a non-combat environment? That is exactly what this book is.

A few days ago a former soldier of mine was complaining on Facebook about not being able to find a job. I messaged him and asked to see his resume. As I perused the documents he sent me, I realized that now that I've been in the corporate world for some time, I look at these things differently. He was an infantryman, a sheepdog, a killer, and now he was trying to find a place in a world that is afraid of guys with his particular skillset. His problem is not unique.

How do we translate what we did? "I was the lead door-kicker on hundreds of raids in the most demanding and dangerous places in the world. I jumped out of planes for fun, trained for hand-to-hand combat twice a week putting my best friends in choke holds, was regularly cold, wet, tired, and hungry. I walked for miles with hundreds of pounds of gear and filled my boots with the blood of blisters. I've buried friends, and sent our enemies to their own deaths. I've been shot at and blown up, and I can bring those skills to your company!" Yeah…no.

I am the first of many of my friends to get out of the army and I regularly give them advice on their transition based on my experience. I have talked to many friends about what they can expect when they get out. I've shown them what pitfalls to avoid, what stats to believe, and how to make those life changing decisions in preparation for your DD 214. We grew up in a different world than most of the people we're going to meet when we get out. We made friendships they wouldn't understand. We made sacrifices they can't believe. We took risks they would never even contemplate, and when we talk about them, we're usually smiling.

In the same way they don't understand us, we don't understand them. How is it ok to be late to work? Why aren't you in my meeting on time? I told you to do this, why are you still sitting there? So you just call in sick like it's no big deal? Don't you have some self-respect? You're crying because a celebrity died? Stop slouching, stand up straight. Stop whispering, do you want me to give a shit about what you're saying? Speak up. If you had a problem with me, you should have come to me. What do you mean you're afraid to give bad news? Some days I just want to scream or start combatives lessons in the grass outside.

All that being said, I've found ways to make this work. In four years in the corporate world I have already been promoted three times into almost a six figure salary. Each time I've taken on a completely different role, and I've been asked numerous times, "how did you go from the assembly line to marketing?!" I've made key decisions in choosing jobs and locations to ensure that I have more opportunities in the future. I've also learned how to interview, how to translate my skills so they're relevant in the corporate world, and how to avoid coming off as R. Lee Ermey.

At the same time I've embarked on one of my toughest challenges to date: learning to be a husband and father. This challenge is harder than being in the Army...in a different way. Now it's more mental than physical. Now I have to fight my emotions, and I don't get to unleash the beast inside. We are trained to maximize violence of action, fight on to the Ranger objective, though I be the lone survivor. Now it's time to put that dog in his cage boys.

The thing is gents, if we walk around the world with this chip on our shoulders, constantly reminding ourselves about how much better we are than the rest of the world, then the world isn't going to give us the time of day. We won't get good jobs, our marriages will crumble, our kids will not become the men and women we want them to become; many of us have already experienced this.

This is not a touchy-feely psychobabble analysis about how you need to be more in touch with your feelings. I'm neither a psychologist nor a social worker. I won't hold your hand or feel pity for you. I hate it when I'm struggling with something and I get that damn sympathetic tone from people. I'm not some fragile porcelain doll that needs a cuddle; get away from me with that bullshit. I'm a fucking killer. I just need some air support right now.

If you are reading this then you are on an obstacle course, I've made it over a few of these obstacles and I'm going to tell you a way of crossing. I'm going to give you real life examples of how to deal with the problems we face. I'll tell you about some of our brothers that have gone through the exact same thing you have and how they were successful. This book is to give you some perspective that can also serve a bit like an FM. I'll teach you some battle drills, but more importantly, I'll teach you how to look at the world around you. I'll show you how to capitalize on the skills you've learned and how to translate your language so the corporate world can understand you.

I'm also going to talk to you about some of the pitfalls the sheepdog falls into with his wife and kids. I've seen far too many tough guys that keep it together at work and then can't be there for the people that matter most. We feel a sense of duty to our family and so we focus on making sure we can bring home the bread, but after a long day of putting forth a façade, we have no energy left to do it at home. Our wives and children get the leftovers, and sometimes not even that. We are quick to anger with them and feel even more betrayed when our partner criticizes us. I really couldn't care less if some douchebag at work doesn't like me, but hard words from my wife really feel like an ambush, and what's the battle drill for that? Right. Don't pretend like you haven't done it.

How do we treat our babies? What do you do when your little boy starts crying? How many of us have told our four year olds to be a man? If you have, then definitely keep reading! Many of us are so focused in ensuring that there is food on the table, then surviving day to day, that we forget that our children need us to be there too. So the folks in the office get the best of us, our wives get the leftovers, and our babies get the scraps. We spend so little time with them, and when we do, it's so hard not to get frustrated when they don't listen, talk back, or don't show respect.

There's still someone that needs taken care of: you. The problem is that I'm telling you that you have responsibilities at work and at home, doesn't seem like there's time for you to take care of yourself. I'll talk to you about some of the things I do to maintain my sanity, and I'll also discuss with you some successful means that guys I know have done.

Although this book details what I went through as a separating Captain, there is still value for those of you that are retiring and are going to pursue your second career and also for those of you who are enlisted and separating voluntarily. Most of the battle drills still apply, even if your particular situation differs from mine.

There is hope, gentlemen. You can be a sheepdog in this world, you can be a leader, you can be a great husband, a dedicated father, a mentor, and you can teach others how to do it too. We can help ourselves and our brothers to keep the 22 veterans from taking their lives each day. Gentlemen, when we decided to take off the uniform, we took on a new mission. This time we didn't have years of training on it, we didn't understand the terrain, we had very little intelligence about the AO, and we didn't understand our enemy. Many of us have found ways of maneuvering in this climate and now it's time for us to share that with you.

Acronyms

1LT- 1st Lieutenant

1SG- First Sergeant

2LT- 2nd Lieutenant

Af-Pak- Afghanistan-Pakistan

AO- Area of Operations

APC- Armored Personnel Carrier (Looks a lot like a tank)

BDU- Battle Dress Uniform (traditional green uniform worn with black boots)

CAS- Close Air Support

CBRNE- Chemical, Biological, Radiological, Nuclear, High Yield Explosive

CIB- Combat Infantryman's Badge

CONUS- Continental United States

CPT- Captain

CQB- Close Quarter Combat

CSM- Command Sergeant Major

ETS- Expiration of Term of Service

FOB- Forward Operating Base

IBA- Individual Body Armor

JTAC- Joint Tactical Air Controller

LTC- Lieutenant Colonel

MAJ- Major

MASCAL- Mass Casualty event

MI- Military Intelligence

MOS- Military Occupational Specialty

Acronyms

MRE- Meal Ready to Eat

NCO- Non-Commissioned Officer (Sergeant to Sergeant Major)

NCOIC- Non-Commissioned Officer In Charge

OPORD- Operation Order (mission plan)

OSHA- Occupational Safety and Health Administration

PCS- Permanent Change of Station

PPE- Personal Protective Equipment

PSD- Personal Security Detail

PX- Post Exchange

QRF- Quick Reaction Force

S1- Staff office of Personnel

S2- Staff office of Intelligence

S3- Staff office of Plans and Operations

SAW- Squad Automatic Weapon (Machine gun also known as M249)

SFC-Sergeant First Class

SGT- Sergeant

SIGINT- Signals Intelligence

SSG- Staff Sergeant

SUPCOM- Support Command

TIC- Troops in Contact

TOC- Tactical Operations Center

TRP- Target Reference Point (used in calling artillery)

UAW- United Auto Workers

WMD- Weapons of Mass Destruction

XO- Executive Officer (2nd in command)

Part 1

Corporate

1. The Decision

The last two years I had taken a cushy assignment in Aberdeen, MD. In my first four years in the army, I deployed two of them and spent the first one in schools, so I was ready for a break. I split my time between a corner office and a SCIF working on counter-WMD intelligence.

Our unit was created after the Iraq invasion when we lost total control of the WMD. I know what you want to say "SO THERE WERE WMDs!!" Well yeah, but not the kind that Bush implied. There were some chemical weapons which we knew were there because we gave them to Saddam. There was also some yellow cake uranium which you can't make a nuclear bomb out of. I'd explain the details, but this isn't the time and place and this isn't a political book. Bottom line is that the Army realized it fucked up when a bunch of infantry dudes kept rolling on forward leaving chemical munitions unsecured for the next enemy to grab up. So, they created the 20th SUPCOM CBRNE. It was a one star general command, and I picked it because it wasn't going to deploy unless we invaded North Korea or some other place like that.

In 2009 when I showed up, it was still a pretty new unit. There were a lot of empty right shoulders which I couldn't believe and it was the first time that I had to work in a joint or sometimes combined environment. For those of you that don't know, joint means different services (Air Force, Marines, Navy, Army) all in the same command, and combined is different countries in the same command. You might recognize the term CJTF (Combined Joint Task Force). I had the chance to get some pretty cool training on chemical, biological, radiological, and nuclear weapons. I also got to work on standing up the first WIT (Weapons Intelligence Team) training course. I learned that although nuclear weapons make the biggest boom, it's the biological ones that are really scary.

Think if someone was able to weaponize the flu and make it deadly. You can't see it, smell it, or taste it, then you die; that would suck. At least with nukes we have a lot of really cool ways of detecting them long before they ever become deadly, and that was five years ago, who knows what other nerdy crap they've come up with since then! Also, let me just hop up on my soapbox really quickly, if we reprocessed nuclear fuel, we wouldn't have to store anymore and we wouldn't have to mine uranium for around another 100 years. We have enough right now to power everything in the US for a century and have a miniscule amount of waste. It's what the French do, go look it up. Blame Jimmy Carter...anyway, moving on...

My branch manager realized that it had been some time since I deployed and they really didn't want to let all that "experience" go to waste. I got my first call in late winter 2011 from a fellow Captain who let me know that it was approaching time to PCS. I was a branch detail officer which meant that the first four years

1. The Decision

in the Army I was an Intelligence officer on loan to the Infantry, then instead of going to the Infantry Captain's Career Course, I went to the MI course. That also meant that I was a ranger qualified MI officer with a CIB and an 82nd Combat patch. They wanted me back to make use of all that infantry knowledge as an MI officer overseas. This time, however, I had a one year old son.

It was a really hard choice to leave the Army. I loved the camaraderie, I loved the challenges, excitement, adrenaline, my brothers in arms, and I was good at it. I just didn't want to miss a year of that little boy's life. When I got back from Iraq on my second deployment, there wasn't anyone around in green ramp for me specifically, so I had a chance to stop and watch others hug their families. I remembered seeing one soldier who had several kids. His youngest boy was around 2 years old and ran away from his father and cried holding on to mommy. It was really heartbreaking to see, and although this young NCO dealt with it really well, I knew I didn't want to do that myself. I didn't want to miss a year of his life, and so I dropped my separation papers.

Oh what a shit-storm that was! My boss was an old Infantry guy as well. LTC Pratt, who we called Leonidas, was a steely eyed ranger originally from Argentina. He was laid back, but probably because no one really dared mess with him and he never got intimidated. He spent a few minutes talking to me about my decision, but unlike every other conversation I would have before getting out, he didn't try and talk me out of it. He wanted to make sure I knew what I was doing and that I was prepared for all the challenges ahead. He also informed me of all the people I would need to talk to before the CG would sign my papers: Command Sergeant Major, G3 Plans and Operations Colonel, Chief of Staff (Colonel), Former Chief of Staff (retired Colonel), and then finally I could schedule an appointment with the Commanding General (CG).

Although I worked on the General's staff, I didn't really interface that regularly with so many full bird Colonels, and I definitely stayed away from the CSM. It was a gauntlet, and I feel like those guys conspired with each other to make sure their message resonated. I stood strong that I wanted to get out, but they did a good job in making me think that I would never find a job, I would lose my home, my family would break up because of finances, and then I'd eventually suck start my Glock. Well, maybe not that extreme, but it was pretty close. They were really effective in scaring me, which drove me to make some decisions later that I could have avoided, but it also helped prepare me in a sense.

I was one of the lucky guys to go through Ranger school before Airborne school which was awesome in many ways. First off, it reduced the risk of getting hurt in Ranger school. Getting hurt is the shittiest way to get kicked out of Ranger school. You still go home tabless and you still have to do everything over again. It's even worse than getting recycled because when you get hurt, you actually get to go home, to the real world, and experience freedom before going back. You sleep in a comfy bed, all warm and snuggly, with a full belly and a recent shower with a smile permanently secured on your face. Except in the back of your mind you know... it's only temporary...the suck is coming.

1. The Decision

I had a good friend in the 82nd that got hurt and showed up without a tab. If you've never been to the 82nd then you wouldn't know, but if you're an infantry officer and you don't have a tab, you're not going to lead troops…generally. Everyone looks down on you, and you have double to prove. My friend Don Bangler took all this in stride. He would later prove to be a real badass when his small two vehicle convoy got near ambushed and his vehicle got high centered in the kill zone. Don led an assault through the ambush and sent the enemy running. Then to further assert his manhood, he called in air support and decimated all of them as they retreated. He earned himself a bronze star with valor that night, and after our deployment, he went back and got his ranger tab and eventually his long tab as

Me (left) and Don

well. He now walks around with a wheelbarrow for his balls.

Another great benefit to being a leg in Ranger school is that you get to take a nap when everyone else is jumping. I know, it seems unfair, and it is, get over it. All of us legs carried the machine guns for the first day in Florida phase, but we were pretty well rested, so we didn't care. Finally, when you do go to Airborne school, you've got a Ranger tab. Let me tell you, when you graduate from Ranger school, you feel invincible, and you actually believe you are. I'm serious, it's the only time in my life that I literally felt like superman. They may break you down, but they build you up twice as strong, which means that I was not going to be intimidated by a black hat. Many of those guys also don't have tabs, so the young ones that want to go will stop you to ask about the course. Airborne school was a breeze.

I remember my first jump very clearly. I'm afraid of heights, seriously, I really am. One of the worst days in Ranger school was the water confidence course because of that damn log walk. I had a good friend run across that thing for a major plus, I wanted to smack him, but I was frozen at the top, so that wasn't going to happen. Anyway, I remember when I got the 30 second warning from the jumpmaster and my heart sank. I had a pit in my stomach as I shuffled to the door staring at the outside. I kept running through everything I needed to do in my mind: look the safety in the eye and hand him your static line, don't throw it, big leap out the door, keep your eyes open, chin on chest, keep control of your reserve handle, good body position on exit…. I jumped out of the plane and did everything exactly as we were trained. Finally, after I checked my canopy and looked for fellow jumpers, the reality of what I was doing set in.

I looked down and saw my legs dangling with nothing below them for hundreds of feet. It was amazing and surreal. The air was quiet and I was alone. I could hear the black hat on the megaphone telling us what to do, but it was more like a muffled sound in the background, I knew I was safe and I couldn't believe what I was seeing. It was a beautiful day in Georgia, there were almost no clouds and the sun was warm on my face. I fell in love… then came the landing. I hit the ground like a sack of shit. My legs crumpled and my ass slammed the dirt hard, right before the back of my head bounced. The wind was knocked out of me and I laid there staring at the sky, mustering up enough energy to pull my canopy release so I wouldn't be dragged across the drop zone. I laid there and smiled as I saw the other canopies above me. It hurt, I could barely breathe, but that was fucking awesome.

Deciding to leave the army was a lot like that first jump. I was scared, nervous, and excited all at the same time. I had no idea what to expect and when I jumped, looking down was surreal, peaceful, and amazing. Then comes the landing and reality jolts you. The biggest difference though, is that in Airborne school someone is telling you exactly what to expect. They go through the possible scenarios of what can go wrong. They tell you what not to do and explain the consequences of every action. You even jump with a reserve parachute in case something does happen, and you know exactly when to pull that handle. When you get out of the Army, you don't get any of that necessary information. Imagine trying to rig a chute and jump it without any training. Chances are most of us would die.

Those of us that struggled when we got out didn't really see it coming, either that, or we figured we could handle it. Many of us make it, we find ways to deal with the problems we created and we chug along, but wouldn't it be nice if someone had trained us up before that jump? If you're thinking about getting out, then I'm glad you picked up this book now! You're thinking ahead, and you're doing better than many of us did. Good job, now let's talk about a few things.

The Four Big Questions

If you don't have good answers to these questions, stop reading and go figure it out!

1. Are your finances in order?

Before you get out, make sure you have zeroed out major debts. I really recommend paying off cars and having as few monthly payments as possible. Take a look at what your monthly expenditures are and make a budget. This will let you know exactly what you need to survive. If that number is equivalent to what you are making in the military (including BAH), then you're spending too much. Chances are, your first job is going to be equivalent to your base pay, if you're lucky, but probably not higher. So you're going to have to learn to survive on just your base pay. You are going to be entering a world where salaries are negotiable, and employers are going to offer you the least they think you will accept, so you need to know exactly how much you need. You and your family are used to living at a certain standard, you're going to start off below that standard, and you need to know exactly what your floor is.

Also, there are taxes to consider. If you're like me, I kept my Florida registration so I didn't have to pay state income tax. Once I got out, that all changed and it was a kick in the nuts to have that extra expense. You're going to have to pay for health care now as well and that's not cheap. There are a lot of unexpected financial hits that you're going to take, and it's best that you're set up to take those punches. If you're not ready now, take a few months, maybe extend out your ETS date if you can so you can get it together.

Here is an example of what happens with my paycheck. Take a look at the deductions and taxes! This is something I certainly

Payment Summary	
Cash Earnings	$ 103,099.00
Deductions	$ 19,231.18
Taxes	$ 21,599.50
Net Pay	$ 62,268.32

wasn't prepared for. About 40% of my paycheck is gone before

I even see it. Some of that goes to pay for my healthcare, some goes into a 401k for retirement, some goes into a dental policy, and some goes into a Health Savings Account or HSA. So if your target salary is $72,000 a year, make sure you're not planning for having $6,000 a month in your bank account, you're probably only going to bring home about $48,000 of that.

For most of you while you're in, your base pay is pretty much equivalent to what ends up in your bank account. If you're deployed you're not paying taxes, and if you're stateside, you have COLA, BAH, and BAS. Once you get out, everything is coming out of that base pay, plus health care costs, plus you're paying for your retirement somehow. I didn't realize this and accepted a lower base salary than I would have if I realized I was going to lose 40% off the top.

2. Do you know why you're getting out?

This is really an important question that gets glossed over by guys. If you're answer is 0400 formations, or my wife hates the military, you might want to think twice and have some tough conversations. I had a clear direction, and years later, that thought still resonates with me. I didn't want to miss a year of my son's life. I now have three kids and I cherish every single second I get to be with them. There is no way I want to go back. If you don't know though, if it's just that you're pissed off at someone above you, or you want to grow a beard...bro...you need to think about this. I've seen several guys get out for the wrong reasons, and then a couple years later regret it. You need to do this for you, not for someone else. If your wife hates the military, you better take some time to soul search and communicate with her because if you get out and then resent her for making you do something you didn't want to do, you're going to lose her anyway and hate her even more. So think about it, know the answer, and make sure it's something that will still be there years to come.

I know it sounds crazy, but you are going to miss the military. Maybe not the first day, or even the first year, but a time will come when you miss the excitement, the adrenaline, and the camaraderie. If you aren't solid on why you got out, it won't go well for you.

For those of you retiring, congratulations, you made it!

3. Do you know where you want to live?

Determining a location is quite difficult because there are tradeoffs to what decision you make. If you decide to be geographically mobile, it will be easier to find a job, but you could end up far away from where you really want to be. If you limit yourself to a particular city, you could be looking for a job for years.

Not only was I in the Army, but I was a Navy brat, so I've always moved around. When it came time to get out, my wife and I talked about location a bit. Remember when I said that those guys had managed to scare me? Yeah, this is one of the areas where it affected my decisions. I knew that if I was open geographically to living and working anywhere, that my chances for getting a job where much better. So I think I talked my wife into agreeing to live anywhere.

It only took 12 months in Ottumwa, Iowa, a town of 30,000 people in the middle of nowhere with blazing hot summers and negative 50 degree wind chills in the winter, for my wife to change that tune. Living anywhere no longer became acceptable. Living 90 minutes from the nearest airport was also unacceptable. We found out we're city folk, and we like malls and shops and eating out and being near a big airport. So we have now agreed that we will retire in her hometown of Tucson, Arizona. In the meantime, we will try to get there.

If we had been honest with each other in the beginning, and if we hadn't been scared into accepting the first job offer we got, I don't think we would have ended up in Iowa. We were effectively scared by the command staff as I was getting out, and I knew that my best chances of finding a job were if I was ok with living anywhere geographically. So I made the decision to accept pretty much any geographical location if the job paid well.

This is an area where you need to consider a tradeoff. If you limit yourself geographically, you're going to lose out on a lot of job opportunities. So consider this carefully and understand that you might be looking for a job for a long time if you are unwilling to move from your current city. If it is really important for you to be close to home, but you also need a job in a hurry, consider a larger geographical area like the Midwest, Southeast, Southwest, Northeast. You might want to be near family in Florida, consider whether Georgia, Alabama, Mississippi, Louisiana, etc. are all options.

If I had started by focusing my search in the Southwest, we would have had many opportunities, and at the same time been closer to home and that would have probably been a better tradeoff. This is not an easy decision, and if you are firm that you refuse to move, understand that I'm not exaggerating when I say it could be years before you find a job.

I'm glad things have turned out the way they have, however. We made the best out of that location, and we met some awesome people. Plus I got a job with a really awesome company, and if I hadn't considered the Midwest, Deere would definitely not have been on my list.

4. Do you know what you want to do?

This is something I didn't know, I wanted to remain open to as many possibilities as possible, and to be frank, I really didn't know what I wanted to be when I grew up; heck, I still don't know. I don't want you to decide to do something that you're comfortable with unless that really is your passion.

"Well, I'm an MP, so I guess I'll be a cop."

No. Stop that shit. Do you *want* to be a cop? If the answer is no, then don't just blindly do something because it was your MOS. Look, I was an infantryman (11A) and an MI officer (35D), since I got out I've been an assembly line supervisor, marketing manager, and now I'm a program manager. Luckily this is one area that I didn't listen to those doom sayers. Just because I had a TS/SCI didn't mean that the best opportunity for me was to work as a DOD civilian. I didn't want to sit around in a SCIF reading intel reports. Your headhunter is a great resource here. Be honest, if you don't know what you want to do, but you're articulate and you know how to spell, then there's a really good likelihood that he's going to be able to find you a job that pays about as much as you make now.

I know you want to make more than you make now. That'll come, and we'll talk about it later, but we need to manage some expectations. You're starting at the bottom again and no one cares that you were a first sergeant or a company commander. What's your first name? That's who you are now; I became Louis, the ex-army guy with no experience. The truth is, you don't know how the real world runs, but that's ok. You bring a special set of skills that are highly sought after and I'm going to teach you how to use them, but before we get into that, answer these four questions.

If you haven't gotten out yet, don't read the next chapter until you have answered the four questions. You're about to make a major life changing decision and you need to check your static line. When you come back to this book, you're going to have a plan for your money, a good reason for getting out, you're going to know where you want to live, and you're going to have a few options on what you want to do. By the way "lead people" is an option.

2. Getting the Job

How many of you, when you were getting out just made a resume off of a Microsoft Word template, threw it up on Monster.com or some other job website and waited for a call? Are you still waiting? There are millions of people doing just that. When I post a job for someone, there are thousands of applicants. I need to somehow screen through all those people to narrow it down to 3-5, then from them I'm going to pick one.

The military doesn't really teach us how to find a job. We walked into a recruiter's office years ago, and he really didn't care what our GPA was, he needed a body and we had one. Most of us have no experience in hunting for a job, and when we ask around our military community, they push us towards the .gov websites. When I got out, I didn't want to work for the government anymore, and I didn't know what to do.

Survival Tip: Find a headhunter

I can't remember how I got the idea, but I started looking around for military head hunters. I found several companies and ended up spending hours on the phone with different groups. When they call you, they're sizing you up to see if you're going to be a good candidate. These companies get paid to find talent by some major corporations, but I haven't heard of any of them saying "no" to a potential applicant. What I have seen is people get a lot fewer interviews.

I finally settled on Lucas Group because I liked the guy that I talked to and they didn't require me to work exclusively with them. Some of the other top companies require that you sign an exclusivity contract with them and not work with any competitors when you're looking for a job. Lucas Group was confident enough in their ability to help me get the best job. It was like they said, "Yeah, go ahead and ask around all you want. You're going to go with us anyway." It felt cocky, and I liked that. Plus the dude that I talked to was a former combat arms guy as well and he understood my language.

I sent Lucas Group my Microsoft Word template resume and they hacked it all up. I wrote it like I was applying for a government job. It was several pages long, wordy, I used too many acronyms, I explained the job too much, and I didn't talk enough about what I did. This is where I learned to write a resume, not in some class as you prepare to ETS (those people have never had to write a resume either). Your headhunter on the other hand, feeds his family on his skills with resumes. These guys are making a living off of preparing guys like you to go out there and kick ass. They have a vested interest in making sure you succeed, and they don't want you to look bad. Take what they say and listen. Don't get defensive when they critique your work, these guys know what they are doing, and the more they hack on your stuff, the better it's going to be, and that means a higher salary later.

Here are some tips to your resume:

1. Try and keep it to one page, no more than two. (If you are separating 1 page, retiring 2 pages)
2. Start with your most recent job at the top.
3. Talk about what you did at that job and use the STAR format- Situation, Task, Action, Result.
4. Make the bullets worthwhile and avoid platitudes. Don't say something like, "was a great leader" or "showed perseverance", that's stupid. Literally every jack-wagon on the planet can find some excuse to put that on his resume. You are better than that. You are better than every one of those idiots, now tell them why.
5. Give specific but *relevant* examples. My resume doesn't say anything about the time I led an assault up a mountain against a superior entrenched enemy force. Instead it highlights the fact that we had zero property loss when I was an XO. Yeah, I know, that's not exciting, but it's what the civvies live for, so give it to them.
6. Make sure you don't have any misspellings, different fonts, misaligned bullets, any of that.
7. Get. A. Headhunter. Once again, these guys are going to make the difference. This is not a book about how to write a resume. I'm only giving you these tips so that your first impression for your headhunter is a good one. That way you get the good interviews.

I have reviewed a lot of resumes of old army buddies. They all suck. As a corporate stooge (like I am now) wouldn't hire any of them; mine sucked in the beginning too. It's ok to not know how to write a resume, it's not ok to settle for that piece of crap and put your livelihood at stake because of it. It's also not ok if you still haven't sat this book down to google military headhunters. Do not make this transition without their help. This is like going on mission without any sort of indirect fire support or air support. That's just asking to get killed. That silly piece of paper is the lifeline to feeding your family, make it a good one and don't get sensitive when someone is helping you to make it better.

Anyway, after I fixed up my resume we did several mock interviews on the phone. Here's another reason why these guys are great. Eddie Commender, who was my Lucas Group rep, helped me translate some of my skills into their corporate relevant counterparts. For instance, in one of our mock interviews he asked me why I was getting out of the Army. I went into some long description about my son and family and all that stuff that I've already told you about. Eddie stopped me, "Listen, that's all well and good, but it makes you sound unhappy, and no one wants to hire someone who's already sour. Try something like, 'it was a great experience but I think I'm ready for a different stage in my life.'" He was spot on, especially now that I've been in this world, that answer would turn me off as a hiring manager as well. I took his answer and made it my own, added some fluff around it and internalized it.

Survival Tip: Read Job postings

This is a difficult skill to learn, especially without experience, but here's something I learned after I was already in the corporate world: read job postings to find out what to talk about in your resume and in the interview. Every job posting is going to give you "desired qualifications", but more than that, read the job description carefully. What is this person really looking for? You're going to notice some underlying trends that you have experience with: leadership, organization, communication, inspiring, planning, presenting, etc. Highlight those skills in your resume.

If you made it out of basic training, I guarantee you're better at every one of those things than 75% of the entire civilian workforce. These aren't the things that you love, nor the things that you tell stories about, "oh dude, this one time I wrote an OPORD that was amazing, and the sand table was perfect!" But guess what, that's actually a really marketable skill. Except most of you don't know how to translate it into corporate talk. If you're able to make a detailed plan, to include branches, organize and inspire a team, communicate and present the plan, then execute on the plan, you're hired. Go ahead and peruse job postings in an area that you think you might like to work in. Identify some recurring themes and key words, then make sure you incorporate those themes and words in your resume and later in your interview answers.

I got the invite from Lucas Group to their Midwest hiring conference. I was about two months away from my ETS date and I was starting to get nervous, so being told that I was finally going to get some interviews was great. I put in my 86 page leave packet and caught a flight to Chicago. Those two days feel a lot like a blur. This was a pivotal moment in my life, and even though I kind of knew that in the back of my mind, it still didn't really set in. It's a lot like when you make the final drive to

Basic Training (OBC in my case). You know it's a big deal, but the reality of it doesn't set in until you're in it.

Survival Tip: Get plenty of rest and stay focused for the next 48 hours, your future depends on it!

The first day of the conference we were given an interview packet that had our schedule and the list of companies that we were going to be interviewing with. Then we sat in a bunch of briefings where we were told about the companies and a little bit about the jobs themselves. I paid close attention, took notes, and asked questions. I made sure to write down some bullet points that I caught about each company. My plan was to research each of them and the areas where the jobs were that night in my hotel room. I was one of a few candidates that had nine interviews the next day. I went from 7 am until 5 pm with a 30 minute break for lunch. That meant that I needed to do all of my preparation the night before, there would be no time for breaks, and I needed to get plenty of sleep, even though I was already nervous.

I heard as we approached the end of the day that John Deere was going to host a beer and pizza event in the hotel bar. Here's the thing, at this point in my life, I was a lot like Frank the Tank when it came to alcohol, so this was going to be quite the challenge for me. When I approached the hotel bar I was cautious. I wanted to make sure that I kept myself under control, and frankly, I had no idea what to expect.

There were three people from John Deere there and the rest of us were applicants. One of the Deere guys was a former Army officer. He was a large gregarious black guy who seemed very entertaining and funny, and most of the candidates for the job had huddled around him. The second person was an older lady who was their human resources manager, and she reminded me a lot of Hillary Clinton. She had those same cold eyes that never matched the smile on her face which felt forced. She and I were getting pizza at the same time and I quickly realized during our exchange of niceties that I really wasn't interested in talking to her. Sitting in the corner at a high top bar table with a beer in hand was Don Crosby.

Don was in his mid-fifties, and although he had a beer belly, you could tell that at some point in his life he was probably a wrestler or football player. He was a pretty quiet guy which is probably why most people were avoiding him. I recognized the bump in his lip for chewing tobacco, then I noticed the signature two beers in front of him: one to drink and one to spit. I decided that I would go and talk to this guy; we had to have *something* in common.

I don't remember much about my conversation with Don except that it went pretty well. He was a really cool guy, and his son was actually in the Army and in special operations. He told me a bit about the job and the area. It was really interesting to hear Don talk about how proud he was to actually be creating something, something useful, and of high quality. He told me a story about seeing some equipment when he went to visit his son in Georgia or something, and he knew that the piece of equipment he was looking at was built on his assembly line, and during his tenure. It was a neat story and one of the few "aha!" moments I've had since getting out of the army.

Survival Tip: Find purpose in your work

I excused myself after about an hour and went back into my hotel room and contemplated what Don had told me in between my research about the companies that I would interview with the next day. This new phase in life meant that I would have to find a different purpose for what I was doing. Being in the army, it was real easy to find meaning and purpose. I decided that I wanted to go chase bad guys in the Afghan mountains to keep my country safe, so everything I did was to hone my skills as a soldier to make sure I was the one putting people in the ground and not my enemy. Every mile I ran, every time I cleaned my weapon, I was always battle focused, and I trained my soldiers that way too. Now, however, that wasn't the case anymore.

A paycheck doesn't really excite me that much. One of my buddies at John Deere would sit and chant, "gotta get that money, money," every time he was faced with a challenge and knew that he was going to be working hard or long hours. That was his motivation, but it didn't really work for me. I like money, and I need it to survive, but I wasn't a soldier for the paycheck. If that was the case, I would've picked a different branch. I wanted to be an Airborne Ranger and get into firefights and kill bad dudes. I refused to ask someone to do something that I was unwilling to do myself, and I loved doing that crazy shit. Don gave me my purpose in the civilian world and he probably never realized it.

I was becoming a creator. For the last seven years I had been a destroyer, and I was pretty damn good at it. Now was the time to create things, and go home knowing that I was actually improving the wealth of my country and helping farmers to put food on all our tables. Having this perspective, and finding out what my piece of this great big puzzle is, made a big difference for me. It also became another way of being patriotic, and today

I sometimes walk around the office and thank people for what they do.

Recently, one of our machines failed an emissions test which meant that thanks to government fiat, there is an entire assembly line of people that will be out of a job in one year. I was tasked with figuring out a way to make sure we could develop an emissions compliant vehicle in less than a year so that we can stay in the business. As I walked into the factory, I realized there are people coming to work and have no idea that I've been busting my ass to make sure they still have a job in a year. I may not feel the same sense of patriotism I did when I wore a uniform, but I can surely hang my hat on the fact that I did some good for a lot of people.

Back to Chicago...The next morning I woke up before my alarm, put on my suit, double checked my schedule and got to work. My memories of the day are hazy at best. I remember sitting with some guys from Fidelity and thinking that being a number cruncher would be super boring. Then I sat with some steel manufacturer in Chicago who's starting salary and commission was about half of every other job and I remember thinking that I was doing that interview as a favor to Lucas Group. I sat with some pretty cool guys from a company called Diageo who makes liquors (they specifically asked for "no douchebags"). I interviewed with Unilever and that was really promising, their interviewers were very good. I remember sitting with Nestle waters and realizing that northern Michigan was no place for a guy originally from Miami.

A little after lunch I walked into my Deere interview, across the table was Don Crosby. I laughed and he stood up and gave me a handshake with a big smile on his face. All that time we sat and talked the night before, he knew he was going to be doing the interview; I picked the right person to hang out with. After Deere I had a few more that I can't remember now, and I ended the day with Rolls Royce. That guy was a former 82nd paratrooper as well and it felt like he interviewed me for five minutes, then we talked about the army for the rest of the time.

By the end of the day, I think I had seven or eight companies say "yes" to me and one or two say "no". It was great because it meant they were competing for me in a sense. I really liked the guys from Diageo, but they needed someone a lot sooner than I could get there, so that was out. I ruled out a few others based on salary, the company itself and whether or not it was stable, and how I hit it off with the interviewer.

Survival Tip: During a recession, pick a recession proof company

I'm sure that the folks at Enron thought that they would be working there for many years, but if a company has been around for a century and is still strong, I'd say there's a good chance they're going to be around for your retirement too. You also don't want to go through all this trouble only to get laid off in a year or two and have to do it again. Unlike the military, you can lose your job pretty fast in the civilian world, so you want to take some time and do some good research into the company you are picking. I eventually narrowed it down to two options: John Deere and Unilever.

John Deere really made a huge impression on me pretty quickly because they offered to fly me *and* my family to Iowa for a second round of interviews. That was pretty huge because my family is my whole world and I didn't want to make a life changing decision without discussing it with my wife. A lot of companies say that they believe in work-life balance and they spew platitudes about the importance of family, but Deere was really showing it by forking out the cash for a couple extra plane tickets.

The morning after we arrived in Ottumwa, Iowa, I began my next round of interviews. I interviewed with the factory manager, two business unit managers, human resource and labor relations managers, and a few others. I also got a factory tour, and they drove me and my wife around the town with a realtor. It was a long day of interviews, again, but by the end of it, I had an offer for a job!

Survival Tip: All your interview answers should be in the STAR format- Situation Task Action Result

This is a good time to pause and talk about how to be successful in interviews and what you can expect. I'm not sure what I thought I was going to see, but just about every question I got from all those different companies started with, "tell me about a time when…" Here's what you need to do:

Pick 6-8 events where you really shined in your career that show skills that can relate to the corporate world, things that highlight your organizational capabilities, communication, planning, leadership, whatever. Try and have more recent examples and fewer older examples. Try to avoid talking about firefights and actual combat, but if you do, tone it down as much as possible (it scares them). For instance say something like, "During an enemy engagement, I was coordinating multiple units from different disciplines. Although it was a chaotic situation, my leadership brought calm and order to a cross functional team. I stayed in control, making decisions, and ensuring we were working together towards the same goal, even though many of us had never met before. I knew how to use each member of the team appropriately and at the right time. In the end, we achieved our objective."

Those of us that have been in combat recognize what it looks like when a leader is in his truck on the radio calling in artillery, air support and maneuvering soldiers while bullets are whizzing by. All I did was take that situation, remove the hooah, add a couple buzzwords like "cross functional" and "working towards the same goal" and I civilianized a firefight without making it seem scary. It shows that I understand the civilian world, I'm capable of sound decision making in even the most extreme environments, but I'm also not scarred and incapable of using that leadership in a non-hostile environment.

Put each of those events in the STAR format. What was the situation, what was your assigned task, what did you actually do, what was the result. Take the example above, it's a loose STAR format, but you probably want to call out each letter before you go into it. Many of these interviewers have a paper in front of them and you make it easy if you tell them what you're talking about. For instance: The situation was that we were called out to assist a patrol that had been engaged by the enemy. My task was to get those soldiers out safely. What I did was [see above], and the result was we brought everyone home. Once again, I don't recommend firefights as an example, but if you must, make sure you have plenty of non-combat related examples as well.

Memorize your examples! I wrote them down in bullet form. Off to the side of each example, I wrote down what qualities they exemplified. Because I'm a visual learner, I was able to recall my paper during the interview. If you want to, you can even take your paper into the interview with you to jog your memory, but I think that slows you down.

Rehearse the answers. If you have several good diverse examples, you should be able to apply them to EVERY question you get.

Make sure you are thinking about the question you were asked however, and you tailor your answer to the question. Avoid using the same example twice in the same interview, but if you're doing a day of panels, it's ok if you use one, maybe two, examples twice.

If you're having trouble remembering moments during your preparation, go pull up old OERs or NCOERs. You can also read some of your award write-ups. I pulled examples from both.

The offer from John Deere was pretty awesome. It was a bit more than my base pay as a captain, and the benefits were great. Here's an area where all the fear mongering from the command staff had an effect on my decision making. I didn't negotiate with Deere at all, I also didn't wait to see what Unilever was going to offer me, in fact, I didn't even go to interview with Unilever. My wife and I made the decision that night that we were going to go with Deere.

It's probably very likely that I would have ended up with the same choice, but there's no way of knowing now because I felt like I needed to make a decision quickly. I also ignored the advice from my Lucas Group representative who said that I should go interview with Unilever before making the decision. He was right.

2. Getting the Job

John Deere is an amazing company to work for. They have excellent pay and benefits, and really take care of their employees. They have also been around for 175 years, so they have weathered a few economic downturns. It was and still is a sure bet, I'm glad I chose them and they chose me.

3. The First Day

North Carolina 2005

I arrived at Fort Bragg within 48 hours of graduating from Airborne school. Although I was excited to see my buddies, I already had gotten a call from the Battalion S1 that the Battalion Commander (BC) was waiting in the office for me to come meet him. I arrived on Friday afternoon after driving straight from Ft. Benning and knocked on the BC's door.

LTC Donovan looked up from his desk without lifting his head, "Report!" I walked in, saluted, and introduced myself. He returned the salute and leaned to his right, looking intently at my left shoulder to verify there was a Ranger tab. His eyes moved from my shoulder and met my eyes, "standby Louis." He picked up the phone and dialed, "Brandon, it's colonel Donovan, your new LT is here…Yes, in my office…ok." He hung up the phone and we exchanged some pleasantries about where I was from and where I went to school until CPT Teague showed up.

Teague and I spoke briefly in the commander's office, then we started the walk over to the company headquarters. On the way

3. The First Day

he explained to me that starting Monday the company was going into the field for platoon live fire exercises and I would be leading my platoon. Understand that I literally just drove onto Fort Bragg for the first time, I had no gear at all except my BDU's, and I didn't know anyone in the company.

We arrived at the company headquarters building and the only people there were the XO, the 1SG and us. We popped our heads in each office as CPT Teague explained who I was. He told the XO that I would be needing his gear to lead live fires in two days, finally stopping in his office to have our initial counseling. As I looked around the office, it didn't take more than a couple seconds to realize the caliber of officer that sat before me. There were pictures of Teague as a Ranger Instructor in Florida phase, best Ranger Competition plaque, and several others from previous units.

As I sat and spoke with CPT Teague, 1LT Brown (the XO at the time) leaned into the office and tossed Teague a beer. I looked up and there was one in the air coming my way. I reacted quickly and snatched it out of the air, the cold can held firmly in my hand. I stared at both of them in awe. "Feel free to open that," Teague quipped as he cracked open his own.

Two days later I met my platoon with a rucksack of borrowed gear and a weapon zeroed at the firing range. We got some briefings about how the exercise was going to go, and the order the platoons would execute on. I had done live fire exercises before, but nothing to this magnitude. I would be directing aircraft, artillery, heavy machine guns, and even a small building for some close quarter stuff at the end.

Over the course of the week we did a dry fire, some blank fires, and finally the live fire at night. It was an amazing experience. I had never seen the .50 cal and MK-19 going at the same time right in front of me as we flanked the objective and the fire shifted in front of us. When we went into the house, the targets were set on balloons so they would fall when they were shot, and the boys of 3rd platoon did an incredible job. My first test with them went off without a hitch, in just a few months we'd be doing the same thing, but it's a lot harder when you're getting shot at.

Iowa 2011

I don't remember my first day at the factory, in fact it felt like the first three months were the first day. Unlike when I started with the 82nd, I didn't have nearly four years of preparation for leading welders on an assembly line. I didn't know anything about agriculture, John Deere, manufacturing, welding, or pretty much anything about my job except how to lead men.

I remember there were several classes that I needed to take just to walk into the factory. I had to take vision and hearing tests, learn about safety gear, buy metatarsal shoes, I had to go through compliance courses and more. I spent a week learning about OSHA regulations and what I took away from it was that it's basically impossible to always be in compliance and don't piss off the inspector because he will shut you down.

I also had to learn SAP. SAP is the software that is used to manage all levels of factory operations. It's a behemoth of a program with hundreds of transactions with weird names like

3. The First Day

MMBE, MD04, ZCWIP, and others. There are subtitles to the transactions that give you some information on what they are for, but you really need to know what you're looking for in order to find it. It took me months to learn how to use the program to any sort of efficiency, and over a year to become proficient.

One of the other key aspects of the job was the United Auto Workers Contract with John Deere. It was a little yellow book with hundreds of pages of legalese that I had to become an expert in. The contract has details about shift times, scheduling overtime, pay, holidays, absences, grievances, discipline and seniority (to name a few). In addition to the main contract, there were also local agreements. In Ottumwa, one of the local agreements is on what they call "nesting".

Nesting means that the worker has rights to his primary work assignment so you can't send him to work somewhere else and put someone in his booth while he's gone. At first this doesn't seem like a big deal, but if someone doesn't show up for work, as a supervisor I would have to juggle several guys all day to make sure I didn't violate the nesting policy because not everyone was cross trained on every job.

I also had to learn the different classifications of jobs. Robotic welders were F2's, manual welders were F1's, fork lift drivers were V20's, and assembler's were K8's. There were many more classifications, but those pretty much covered our assembly line. In addition, workers had primary and secondary classifications, and because of the seniority clause, they could choose their shift or bid on different jobs within the factory.

All this being said, inevitably something happens where the employee feels that you violated the terms of the contract and files a formal grievance against you. It happens a lot; I got six of them in one day from the same guy who I pissed off the day prior. There's a process for grievances as well, and pretty much any time you discipline someone, they will file a grievance on it. In two years on the assembly line, I became pretty adept at the terms in the contract, and it saved me more than once.

I also had to learn about material flow. In one end of the factory trucks deliver sheets of steel. Those sheets get cut and bent, then moved to a holding area. Then the parts get moved to the assembly line where they are either welded or bolted onto a frame in a gray state. Then the machine gets painted and goes through a second assembly process. All the while there are quality checks throughout and when defects are found they have to be fixed.

There are ways of moving, storing, and presenting material that are more effective than others. Keeping work areas clean, organized, and safe is a priority. Making sure that we are building to the assembly plan so that the line remains balanced and moving is paramount. We will be getting parts according to the schedule and if we stray too far ahead of schedule we'll run out.

Gentlemen, I can go on about the nuances of manufacturing, and I have only scratched the surface here a little bit, but I wanted to highlight how little I really knew about the world out there. When I say you're going to have to start at the bottom, I say so because you don't know any of this stuff, and I didn't even start talking about the customer and the customer needs.

You don't know the business, so you're not going to start in senior or even middle management, there is a ton for you to learn before you will be ready for that. This was something I didn't realize when I first got out. I had led hundreds of men in the most dangerous places in the world, I didn't understand what was so hard about leading 18 welders in Iowa. It wasn't until I began the work that I realized why I had to start at the bottom again.

Starting with John Deere was a lot like my first week with 3rd platoon, except with no training beforehand. I stumbled a lot early on, both with the welders and also with the paperwork portion of my job. The labor relations manager told me one day, "Louis, I don't care if you make mistakes, just make sure they are new and unique ones every time." That is the corporate version of the same sage advice given to me by my Platoon Sergeant SFC Anderson years earlier when we met, "It's ok to step on your dick every once in a while, just don't mark time on that fucker."

Survival Tip: Learn everyone's job

It's ok if you have to take a lower ranking job with less responsibility than you're used to, that's an opportunity to learn the business; take it. Push yourself to learn your job well, then the jobs of your peers, then the jobs of your boss, of all your support staff, etc. I was told by a wise senior Engineer in Ottumwa, "You manage what you know." He was and is absolutely right, so the more jobs you know, the stronger you will be as a manager.

One thing I have noticed within Deere, and I assume that it's true throughout the business world, senior managers are not one trick ponies. Nearly every single senior staff member I know, which would be the equivalent of a Lieutenant Colonel and above, has worked in two or more differing career fields.

In addition to your leadership skills, zeal, and other highly sought after qualities, the key to getting promoted is selecting new and diverse positions. This is an advantage of starting at the bottom because you are more likely to get hired into a new career field with little experience at a lower level.

Imagine you had three or four different MOS's and the military recognized them all equally. You could compete for assignments in every one of those MOS's and you could get selected for promotion in any one of those MOS's. Do you see how it's an advantage now?

So don't get bummed that you're starting at the bottom, use it as an opportunity to strengthen your position in the future. I've been with John Deere for four years and I've done jobs in Operations, Marketing, and Program Management. That is the equivalent of having three completely different MOS's. Also, because of the combined experience of all three, I can realistically apply for positions in Order Fulfillment, and maybe even Quality or Supply Management if I took another lateral instead of a promotion.

All of that means that I can look for jobs in every one of those categories and be very competitive. It means that I can start being more picky about geography than I could before. It also means that I've met people and made connections all over the company in different fields in different states.

Survival Tip: In order to move up, you need to move sideways

3. The First Day

If you're working for a big company, and have aspirations to move up, you need to move sideways first. Do so quickly and make bold leaps that other people wouldn't normally think of doing. It makes you unique and more valuable.

If you still think that I'm full of it and just trying to garnish the shit sandwich of starting at the bottom, go look up the biographies of the directors of your company, or look up CEO's that started at the bottom in their companies. If you don't have the genius of Elon Musk or Bill Gates, and you're going to have to grind your way to the top, your best bet is to be a Jack of all trades so you can be on the field in every play and become an invaluable asset to your company.

I realized this while I was still in my first position and I began to do some research to figure out which functional areas I could compete in with a History degree. I also wanted to take a look at areas that were geographically flexible to increase the chances that I could get a transfer to Arizona. I used this information to focus my efforts in getting a marketing job.

Since I had no experience in marketing, I spoke face-to-face with the local marketing manager and I volunteered to do extra work for him if he needed it. Not many managers will admit it, but the moment you express interest in a job, that's when your interview starts. I used this to my advantage and put forth the best effort I could on the tasks I was given. The moment a position opened up, I was given the opportunity to apply for the job, and ultimately I got it.

Survival Tip: Who you know is just as important as what you know.

Two years later, I applied that same formula once more. I recognized the versatility of being a program manager as a stepping stone and career advancing move. It is a good way to get exposure to all the major functional areas, and also I realized that I would be spending a lot of time in front of leadership. Having a director or a vice-president as an ally when applying for a job is like having an extra queen on the chess board: you're almost guaranteed victory.

I found the manager of program managers one day when she was visiting our factory. As a marketing rep, I played a big part in being the voice of the customer when we were having talks about the next program John Deere was going to pursue. She was vaguely familiar with me when I volunteered to lead a program in addition to doing my duties as a marketing rep. It meant a lot of late nights and long hours, but I managed to make the program work, and just a few months later, I got a full time job as a program manager.

My favorite part of program management is that everything I work on is stuff that isn't in the marketplace yet. I get to work with the big head great idea engineers and find ways to change the marketplace with new equipment; it's really cool. I can do something that is exciting, that is similar to jobs I had in the military, and it opens up even more opportunities in the future.

So once you do some analysis on which career field you want, with laser focus on that task, and a little bit of extra work, you can get ahead of all the other guys that are going to apply when a job opens up.

4. Do what I say

Afghanistan 2005

When we arrived at the base of the mountain to link up with my company commander, my small crew of 11 guys fit in a single cargo HMMWV. We had just been in a heavy firefight a couple days earlier on this same mountain and we were eager to get those bastards again. Captain Teague pulled me aside as I hopped out of the truck. I could see the 120mm mortars getting set up and his small command crew, but everyone else was out of sight. The distinct distant hum of the predator could barely be heard, and the JTAC was off to the side huddled by a tree staring at his computer screen.

"Here's the situation," Teague started to tell me, "we've got anywhere from 40-60 guys on top of that mountain. I've got 1st platoon and an ANA platoon on this ridgeline here." He pointed to my right and I followed his hand to that location. The ridgeline was in an upside down "J" shape and we were in the middle. There was far too much vegetation to be able to see the guys, but I got the general location. "I have the 120's setting up, and we've also got some Apache's on the way. We've also got predator coverage for a while, and the JTAC is looking to find out what other CAS he can get." I nodded as he continued, "I'm going to need you to take your guys up this part and clear the summit."

"Um…sir…I've only got 11 guys."

"I know."

"Isn't it supposed to be three to one odds in our favor?"

"You've got plenty of combat multiplying assets."

I laughed, "Alright sir!"

To understand that interaction fully, you really need to understand Captain Teague. He was a green to gold guy who once was a Ranger Instructor in Florida phase. He also finished the best ranger competition, and earned a silver star during that same deployment. He was a guy that expected all of his officers to score at least a 300 on their PT test, a dedicated father, husband, and a mentor. He truly cared about his soldiers, sincerely. He is a lot like Winters in Band of Brothers and he inspired all of us Lieutenants to really live up to his example and expectation. I trusted him fully with my life, and as I write this, I realize that I probably still do.

As I turned around my squad leader SSG Johnny Walker walked up to me. Johnny was named after the liquor under which he was conceived. He was another badass who loved to carry a LAW rocket on his back and was an expert marksman. I don't mean the kind that hit 37 on a static range, I mean the kind that will take a knee when bullets are flying, look through his ACOG and hit a moving target that is shooting at him 100 meters away square between the eyes. That's not some cool description of a hypothetical, I saw him do it…on his first shot.

"So what's the plan?" He asked as we walked towards each other. "We're going up and clearing the top," I responded still in disbelief and smiling. "What? Are you fucking serious? What the hell is 1st platoon doing?" His voice hit another octave and his hands flew out to his sides. I pointed up to the ridgeline, "they're up there in a blocking position." I smiled at him, "You wanted to get these guys right? Let's go." He scoffed and shook his head. He stood there looking at me for a second, still in disbelief, then he broke a smile, chuckled and turned around. "We're going up boys!" Johnny hollered at the rest of the soldiers in the cargo, "all I have to say is: there are some addresses on my white board in my hooch next to the letters…who wants a cigarette?"

This was a defining moment in my Army career. As I stood there staring at my men smoke their cigarettes, check their weapons and ammo, and actually laugh and joke with each other, I realized that I was among modern-day Spartans. These men were facing a superior enemy force that was entrenched in the high ground and they were joking about who was going to send the letters back home. I am reminded of the story Herodotus writes in Thermopylae of the Persian spy who saw Leonidas and his men preparing for battle against Xerxes' army. The report was that they were oiling their skin, brushing their hair, and telling jokes. They were unafraid and unintimidated; it was men like that who I had the chance to lead!

Iowa 2011

I was a supervisor of an 18 man weld team in the factory. My job was measured by our ability to maintain schedule, quality, efficiency, and safety. Unlike the Army, when you're in a factory with United Auto-Workers, you can't do any "bargaining unit work". That means you can't pick up a part, or a tool, or a tote, or even a screw. If you do, the union can file a grievance on you and eventually you can lose your job. This means that the whole "lead from the front" is much harder to do. I used to do everything my soldiers did to show them that I would never ask them to do something that I was unwilling to do myself. That was my greatest tool as a leader and it gave me some allowances when I was a hardass. In the union world, I was just a hardass.

It took me some time to figure out how to lead that team, and really, after doing it for two years, I'm not sure I completely figured it out. I learned how to survive in that environment, but I started out wrong and it was hard to make up for that.

I was used to soldiers who listened to orders and executed efficiently. On one of my first days as a weld supervisor, I told an employee that he needed to work outside of his regularly assigned area. Every day someone in the factory isn't showing up for work. It is one of our duties to understand what job everyone is capable of doing and flexing the manpower around to make sure we are still building machines to schedule. Sometimes we have to work overtime to make up for it, but the better you are at reacting to the unforeseen absenteeism, or even predicting it, the easier your life will be.

Ten minutes after I had told a specific welder to flex into another booth, I walked by and saw that he was still not where I told him to be. I turned around in a rage and headed right for his booth around the corner. When I saw him he had his weld cape on and was applying sunscreen to his ears and neck and laughing with a buddy (welders can get sunburn if they don't wear sunscreen). This was a heavy set guy with a ZZ top style beard that he had to roll up in rubber bands under his helmet so it wouldn't catch fire. I yelled at him to get moving, and I did it loudly so everyone could notice. I'm not sure what I was thinking, nor why this bothered me that much. I'm not sure if I wanted to show that I wasn't intimidated or what. What I do know now is that it was a huge mistake.

Survival Tip: Chill out, bullets aren't flying, people aren't dying. Take it in stride bro.

That welder was one of my best guys who showed up every day, worked hard and took all the overtime you offered, but I didn't know that then. I was still walking around with that chip on my shoulder like I was better than everyone else and I didn't realize that I still didn't even know the job yet. I was acting as if I was training a bunch of soldiers to attack an objective, and I had no clout whatsoever with those guys. In fact, there is a stereotype that ex-military guys will do exactly what I did. They just come in and yell and scream and have no idea what's really going on or how to run a business. I really didn't know how to run that business, and even worse, I didn't know how to lead those men.

You're not better than everyone else.

You have a different set of skills, and you may be braver, but you're not better. When you understand that, you will stop treating everyone like you're special and instead start treating them like they're special. It was easy to respect those men on that mountain, they were exhibiting traits that I value and think highly of. In the corporate world it's different. Some days I want to punch some people in the face, and when they act like a wimp or whiny it pisses me off. I often have to remind myself that I'm not better than these people and remember that there is probably something that they can teach me. I cared about the men I served with overseas, and I still do. They will always have a special place in my heart and I still speak to many of them regularly. That was something that made me a good leader, now I needed to show some concern for the men in this weld area as well.

Jeremy Barker, my union steward at the time, had a major positive effect on me. I treated him a lot like a platoon sergeant, even though that wasn't his role. He taught me how to lead in a corporate environment, but there was never that camaraderie like the one an officer develops with his NCOIC. My union steward was not my battle buddy, and he made sure to make that clear. Our relationship was a professional one, but he was a guy that understood the business. He taught me how to anticipate problems, where to go looking for them, and when to expect certain people to behave a certain way. He was a bit like a sensei asking questions at the right time.

When I softened my approach a bit with the team, and focused on understanding the contract and living by it, things started to go a bit more smoothly. Eventually I was able to help my union steward get a promotion along with three other men that worked for me. I also helped one of them apply for college and just recently he earned his bachelor's degree. One of my guys even ran for local office and won. I found that I had to adapt my leadership style, but the key wasn't much different: just give a damn about the people working for you. It's really hard to care about someone when you think you're better than them.

These people are not much different than you. They have families that they love and are trying to support. If you really are the great leader you're supposed to be, then you should be inspiring to them as well. Whereas you inspire soldiers through acts of courage, you inspire civilians through acts of kindness. You don't have to be weak to be kind. Think about some of the ways you showed your soldiers you cared about them, when you genuinely cared about them. Now do that.

5. Are you serious?

Afghanistan 2005

Once every two months, one of the platoons in our company would get sent back from Camp Tillman, a remote outpost on the Af-Pak border, to FOB Salerno, a large airfield with three hot meals a day, a small PX and even a Subway by the time we left. We

Me, SPC Butler and SGT Moore

would split the platoon up in two groups: One was the battalion commander's PSD (Personal Security Detail) and the other was QRF (Quick Reaction Force) for FOB Salerno. My platoon drew the short straw and got stuck on QRF duties during the first Afghan elections in 2005. It was a mess.

We were getting called out constantly, a firefight here, a rocket attack there, an IED over here, a MASCAL there. After one particular stint, it had been three days since we had been inside the wire and gotten any sleep. We were all exhausted, and I

5. Are you serious?

remember my driver almost falling asleep on the way back to the FOB. I stopped before I entered the TOC to debrief and noticed I was covered in dirt, grime, and blood. I remembered the story of one of my buddies getting yelled at by the CSM for having his boots unbloused after a firefight. I shook my head as I bloused my boots and straightened my uniform before going in the building; there was nothing to be done about my three day beard.

Luckily the sergeant major wasn't around as I wrote up my debrief and I got out of there without a hitch. As I was walking out I heard my name called. The assistant S3 stopped me to tell me that they were having a rocket drill that night. "Do you need me for that sir?" I asked. "Yep, you and your men are part of the drill aren't you?" My eyes narrowed, but I knew better than to say what was going through my mind. Here was this recently showered fobbit turd, who could clearly see that I haven't slept in days telling me to be in the command center for a drill in two hours. I could smell the stink of Pantene on him and we both knew that the closest thing he had ever been to combat was at the X-Box in his room. As far as the world was concerned, he and I were both infantry officers in the 82nd airborne and were deployed to Afghanistan at the same time. A note to any civilians reading this: Not all veterans are created equal. Anyway, I gave him a quick, "roger that" and strolled back into the TOC. I looked at the battle captain, a fellow 1LT who knew exactly what we were doing for the past few days and asked him to just check the block on calling the QRF so my guys and I could actually get some sleep. He agreed to arbitrarily check the block and only call us if some real-world event happened.

I strolled back to my hooch, got a shower, laid down on my crappy cot, and fell asleep cuddled by my beautiful woobie.

What felt like 5 minutes later, my ICom radio chirped, "EXERCISE, EXERCISE, EXERCISE. QRF, QRF, this is White Devil 71." I had one eye open, staring at that little black radio wondering what went down that made my fellow LT decide to go all blue falcon. "This is QRF, go ahead," I'm sure my sarcasm and lack of enthusiasm was palpable on the radio. He went on to start to tell me something about a rocket attack, but I wasn't listening. As I sat up on my cot and began to put my feet into my boots I heard the familiar sound of the water bottle sliding up the tent wall as the door was swung open.

SSG Carrol was standing in my hooch machine gunning every curse word he knew and he was quickly joined by the other squad leaders. I explained to them that they didn't need to get out of bed. As far as I was concerned, the men had their gear on and were in the bunkers next to the vehicles ready to execute the counter-rocket mission…or at least that was what I was going to report. As I explained this, my PSG showed up in full battle rattle and a huge smile on his face, "In all my years I haven't seen such seriously fucked up bullshit, Louie, so I'm coming with you to witness this cluster fuck in person."

SFC Steve Anderson was an intimidating human being. He stood at around six feet and weighed about 210 lbs with zero body fat. The guy could bench press 300 lbs and run two miles in 11 minutes. He dipped Copenhagen snuff and didn't have a straight tooth in his mouth. He was also part Native American and shaved his head. During a firefight earlier in the year one of our soldiers was injured and two men were carrying him. SFC Anderson booked it over to them and threw the guy on his back. He then ran with the injured soldier to the LZ while the other two guys pulled security and struggled to keep up. He was a beast.

I pulled the laces on my boots tight, tucked them in to the sides and stood up slowly. I was still half zombie as I got my body armor on and told the squad leaders once again to go lay down. Steve and I walked out of the tent and started walking towards the TOC as my radio chirped again, "QRF, QRF, this is White Devil 71." "This is QRF, go ahead," I answered. "The exercise is over have a good night," I recognized my buddy's voice. He had waited until the last second to call and probably got asked directly whether or not he had called me. Turned out he wasn't being a blue falcon, he was trying to look out for us. Then the radio chirped again, "Good! Maybe someone can get some fucking sleep around here!" SFC Anderson and I looked at each other in disbelief. I stood there staring at the little black box in my hand as if looking at the radio was going to give me some answers. "Bravo 36 this is White Devil 3A," the assistant S3 used my specific call sign. "This is Bravo 36," I responded. "Come to the TOC to receive your ass chewing." I laughed, Steve laughed, and I could hear Carrol laughing in his tent as well. I took a deep breath, answered with a cool "roger" and headed towards the TOC.

Steve looked at me, "Oh this is too good! I want to see this fucker chew some ass! Let's go." We walked quickly in the dark towards the command center, chatting with one another about who it might have been on the radio. The smart money was on Carrol, but we weren't going to find out until I got yelled at. The more we talked about it, the less patient SFC Anderson got.

Inside the double doors at the command center there was a long hallway. The staff offices were to the left, the TOC itself was on the right and had two doors, finally at the end were the CSM and Commander's offices. The assistant S3 stood at the far end of the hallway with his arms crossed. As soon as he saw me he began, "Why are you saying stuff like that on the radio? Don't you know the commander is in the TOC during those drills?" His tone was even but loud. Immediately anger boiled inside, emboldened by the ten minute conversation I had just had with my platoon sergeant.

"Yes sir, I know, but I didn't say that."

"Then who did?"

"I don't know. I was in the process of finding that out when you called me up here to 'get my ass chewed.'" I did overly dramatic air quotes to show my disdain for this entire activity. The next thing I knew I felt a sharp pain in the back of my leg. SFC Anderson had reared back and kicked me in the back of my thigh almost bringing me to the ground. He then grabbed the back of my IBA collar and lifted me off the ground so only my tiptoes were touching the floor. He looked at the assistant S3, "I got this one sir, let me square away my LT," he said as he spun me around towards the exit. My feet barely touched the ground as he pushed me down the hallway and out the door. I could hear the captain as we walked out, "Alright sarnt' you got this!"

As he pushed me out the door, I spun around like I was going to do something, knowing full well that this was a battle I would surely lose but it was worth the fight. "What the fuck was that for?" I yelled at Steve. "Screw that guy, he's an asshole. Let's go to bed." His big arm wrapped around my head like he was going to give me a noogie followed by his deep baritone laugh as he pushed me forward. Even though I could still feel the sting in my leg, I had to smile; I had the coolest damn Platoon Sergeant ever. Steve was a guy who really did want me to succeed and he put himself in uncomfortable situations to further my career and ensure my success. I tried to do the same for him, but let's face it, he had a whole lot more to offer me than I him. I don't feel like I will ever be able to repay him for what he has done for me.

Iowa 2012

"None of that happened."

Those were the words of one of my employees during a discipline hearing. This was a guy who was notorious for his poor performance. When he worked on third shift he was caught hiding in a box and sleeping during his shift. When he came to first shift to work for me, I always found him outside of his weld booth talking to someone. He took about an hour to get started in the morning, and easily took an extra 10-20 minutes at every break.

At John Deere in UAW facilities they have a performance pay system called "CIPP" or Continuous Improvement Pay Program. To try and explain the system in this short book would be impossible, and really not the point of telling this story. As a supervisor it was one of the hardest things to grasp, but the gist is that the harder the employees work the more they get paid. There are a lot of intricacies in how their performance is measured and exemptions etc., but a key to this system is that their performance is measured as a team. So if you have one guy on the team who is slacking, then the entire team suffers. This means that if you get a dirt bag, generally the entire team starts to slack off because they don't really want to exert themselves if they aren't going to get paid for it. My team had a couple of slackers, and it was part of my job to find new and unique ways to motivate the group to increase their performance. I found a few techniques that seemed to bear fruit, but this particular guy was a thorn in my side.

On this day this guy was in a special mood. He took forever to get his safety gear on to get to welding, and when I mentioned that to him he made a face and I knew it was going to be a long day. I caught him later on that morning talking to someone out of his area with his eye protection off. I walked up and explained to him that this was a safety violation and per the contract he needed to keep his gear on. He turned and looked me straight in the eye, stuck his head out towards me and slowly lifted his glasses off his head and onto his face throwing his hands out into the air after he did. Then he rolled his eyes.

There have been a few times since I left the army that I've wanted to go ape shit knife hand; this was one of them. I could feel the adrenaline start to build up, in the same way you get the rush right before you go into a building or jump out of a plane. I recognized the beast, that animal I've kept caged since I took off the uniform. I could see myself kicking the back of his left leg at the knee, bringing him down as I put him in a rear naked choke and putting him to sleep. I wanted to be violent, I wanted to hurt him. I knew I could do it and this guy was more than deserving of a good ass beating.

5. Are you serious?

This is something most of us never talk about, but deal with every day. That rage that builds so fast, and our mind and body react like it was another battle drill. Without a thought you immediately decide how to neutralize the threat until it doesn't exist anymore, and in this case the guy wasn't even a threat, he was just a dickhead. I managed to keep my inner beast under control and I turned and walked away.

Survival Tip: Silence is your friend, especially when you're angry

I went back to my desk and documented the conversation in great detail. The first time I wrote it down, I added all the flowery language I wanted and I think I wrote "fuckhead" when describing him in the report. I knew I wasn't going to send it out, but it served to help me calm down and even laugh:

0915- Fuckhead is seen without proper PPE by supervisor

0916- Supervisor instructs fuckhead about the appropriate PPE for his current activity....

I still laugh now thinking about it. I later changed it, obviously. In my years in the corporate world I've found that writing really does help me. It often feels like I'm taking that angry beast and putting him on the paper where he will stay. Usually I delete my rants because I don't want anyone to accidently stumble upon my uncensored thoughts, but now that I think about it, it might be good therapy to read my angry musings every once in a while.

Anyway, I caught him two more times later that same day and documented every detail of the event. I finally called labor relations and informed them that I wanted to pursue discipline for a safety violation. If you try and pursue discipline after the first, or even the second event, chances are it's going to get thrown out. Three times on the same day, however, are considered pretty much a slam dunk. I printed out my detailed account of everything that had happened and took the employee to the front office. When we arrived, he was instructed to sit in a conference room and wait for his union representative. In the meantime myself and the labor relations rep, Ryan Moode, went over the events of the day. With my detailed account in hand, I saw this as a sure thing.

We finally started the meeting in the conference room. Ryan brought a tape recorder, as is customary, and began the proceedings. It's all a very formal process. He asked me to explain my version of the events of the day so I pulled out my paper and began to read it. It took almost ten minutes to read the minute by minute account, along with small reenactments of his eye rolling and general smartassery. When I was done, the Union Committeeman looked at the employee in disbelief. That's when it happened.

Fuckhead looked me right in the eye and said, "none of that happened."

I was a millisecond from losing my shit and even took a deep breath to unleash my tirade. I simply couldn't believe that someone would be so blatantly dishonest, it just baffled me. Luckily Ryan Moode, the former cage fighter turned labor relations rep, lifted his hand giving me the "halt" hand-and-arm-signal and I stopped in my tracks. He reached out quickly for the recorder, "we're going to take a recess," and stopped the recording. He looked at me calmly, "Louis. My office." We both walked out of the room and I was in a rage.

5. Are you serious?

Here's the part that really sent me over the edge: they started an investigation to determine which of us was telling the truth! Let's get one thing straight, this guy was about to be disciplined for the 4th time in three years. He was a known liar and a problem for every team he had worked with; he was found hiding in a box during his shift for Christ's sake! Regardless of that, they were basically saying that his word carried as much weight as mine.

Here's one thing that ex-military leaders have over the civilian population, if nothing else, you damn sure better have some integrity. Only a coward has a reason to lie, and we aren't cowards. They made me stand outside of the HR offices as they pulled in my employees to make a determination on which one of us was telling the truth. I couldn't believe that they were questioning my integrity, and in almost five years working for Deere, this was hands down the worst day I've ever had; nothing else comes close. I'm pretty sure that if I wasn't married with two kids, I would have quit on the spot and found another job. They kept assuring me that they weren't questioning my integrity, but if they felt they needed to conduct an investigation, then they're saying there's a chance that everything I wrote was a lie.

After a few hours they determined that everything I said was true (no shit right?) and the employee was suspended for 30 days. I decided that day that I needed to get a different job within the company where I wouldn't be put in that situation again because it did not make financial sense to quit. This is something that the civilians won't understand about us and our culture. We come from a world of principle, where values matter, and when you say something, you mean it. One more time, lying is an act of cowardice and I'm no coward.

Survival Tip: Don't yell

Once you're out, don't ever yell again. Not to your employees, not to your kids, not to your wife, never. You're done with that. Ok, I know it's going to happen sometimes, but you need to try and never do it again. Like I said, there are days when I want to go knife-hand ape shit on some idiot, but that isn't going to get my anywhere. People in the civilian world do not respond to that in any way. The few times that I have lost it, I've had to go back and apologize for it.

You also lose your position of power when you yell. These people look at your background and immediately think about Hollywood's version of a drill sergeant. They expect you to come in throwing desks and putting people in a choke hold, when you raise your voice, that's what they see.

You're also intimidating to them. I know for us, that doesn't really exist, but it's real in the civilian world. We know that there are different types of deployments, and that a finance guy who deployed to Qatar is not the same as the batt boy who was kicking in doors in Afghanistan for 6 months. We also know what it takes to earn some of those hooah badges, and although we have respect for someone that made it through the hell that is scuba school, we're not intimidated by that guy. In fact, most of us look at those guys and wish we would have had the chance to go, or wouldn't have done that stupid thing that got us kicked out, but we definitely don't think they're scary people.

5. Are you serious?

You have to understand that these people don't live in a world where consequences for their actions are swift and immediate. It took two seconds for the Assistant S3 to call me up to get my ass chewed, but "fuckhead" was on his fourth discipline and still has one or two more chances to screw up before he finally loses his job. Granted, a lot of that has to do with the union, but everywhere you look someone is trying to pass the blame to avoid the consequence. They don't like to assume responsibility for their actions; it's always someone else or something else's fault. It was a "wardrobe malfunction" or Hillary Clinton with "what difference does it make." I read in the news the other day about a guy who was taking photos up girls' skirts who later said he had a nervous twitch that made it look like that's what he was doing when really he wasn't. There's one of my all-time favorites that those of us around in the 90's remember, "If the glove don't fit, you must acquit!"

We're coming from a world where you put your sock on the wrong spot of your poncho during an inspection and you're getting your ass smoked. We treat every single activity with the upmost importance because it's that kind discipline that will generate expert warfighters, which means you live and the other bastard dies; that's a good deal in my opinion. People are soft and they expect to be catered to. They think their feelings are products of their external environment instead of their internal thought processes. Every one of them is trying to be a victim of something and they pride themselves off of this victimhood, it defines them and makes them special. I've heard them being called "cry bullies" and it seems very fitting.

In order to business in this world, however, companies need to make concessions and conduct training for its employees to be successful. John Deere selected me to be a part of a new initiative teaching a class about diversity. I think some of that may have been because my last name ends in "ez" but also because my schedule was light on the day the training was supposed to go. I remember how excited the lady that taught the class was about the subject matter. She really believed in this stuff and was making a concerted effort to help us learn to teach it. I participated in all the silly games we had to play and even took notes to be able to teach it myself. When the time came for me to do it, apparently I missed the entire point of the class. When I taught it I minimized the importance of our differences when I should have been highlighting them. There's now a group of John Deere employees walking around who got a completely different class on diversity.

I approached it just like the military. We might all be from different walks of life and different backgrounds, but we all bleed red, and we bleed red for each other. That is the bond that makes our friendships special. I was watching a silly TV show a few months ago and one of the characters said, "He's not my brother. Our relationship is not solidified by something as trivial as blood. Our brotherhood is stronger than that, it's by choice." I sat up in my seat and immediately texted it to three guys; my brothers by choice. So when it comes to making a big deal about diversity my eyes roll back so far that I can see my frontal lobe. It's just a product of a society where every little thing is "offensive".

In order to survive in this world, we must cater to it. We have to be very careful about the battles that we choose to fight. This is where we enter a world of ambiguity. I think of this much like the game of Chess. If you're any good at the game, you think not only about the move you are making, but also about the next move you're going to make and maybe even the one following. If you're a master at the game, you're thinking several moves ahead not only for your side, but for your opponent's side as well. This is how you're going to have to approach conflict in the corporate workplace. You will be sacrificing a lot of pawns in order to get the king.

Here is one way to approach these situations:

1. Start by taking a deep breath
2. What do you seek to gain from fighting this battle?
3. What can go wrong?
4. Do the potential consequences outweigh the potential gains?
5. If so, move on

We are no longer living in a world where everything is life and death; we need to stop treating it that way. If John Deere builds one less machine today, no one is going to die. So what if that guy was disrespectful, my overreaction to assert my position of authority is only going to damage my reputation. People are already extra sensitive to everything you do since they expect you to be a drill sergeant...don't give them the pleasure.

6. The Modern Man

Afghanistan 2005

We found ourselves quickly surrounded and outnumbered. I had radio communications long enough to call in troops in contact right before they dropped off. There were more than twenty of them and only nine of us, and they were attacking us from all sides. We were performing a textbook break contact battle drill while fighting our way up the 10,000 foot mountain. Bullets were whizzing all around, tree limbs were exploding, and rocks were bouncing into the air. We had only been in country a couple months, and my body still hadn't gotten accustomed to the lack of oxygen at this elevation. I was struggling to breathe and move with all the gear, and I could see that my men were as well.

I instructed my forward observer (FO), who on this particular day was carrying the radio, to keep moving up the mountain until he could reestablish comms. I figured the terrain was affecting our ability to communicate, and without comms, we were fighting on our own. In the meantime, we would slow the enemy advance and stay in between him and them. As he stood up to move I heard McKenna yell, "back blast area clear!" and I barely had time to get out of the way before the LAW rocket was on its way. I looked ahead to guess what he was firing at and saw three guys behind a large rock, not too far away. The rocket couldn't have traveled further than its arming range before hitting the rock right in front of us in a huge explosion. The concussion rattled in my helmet and it seemed that for 2-3 seconds, not one person in this battle was firing a round.

I started directing the soldiers to move, Johnny and I were bounding between fire teams, identifying enemy locations and directing fire as we moved. I remember thinking to myself "run asshole!" but I just didn't have the energy to do it. I was a slow, walking, very visible, very out in the open target, luckily those guys have the aiming skills of a junior storm-trooper because not one round found me as a target.

SGT Zimmerman, SPC Kirkland, PFC Smith, PFC Mignone (top center), SSG Walker (bottom center), Me, SGT Harrell

As I made my way up the mountain I saw my FO leaning up against a tree, out of breath but listening to the radio. I asked him if he got comms and he nodded in affirmation. I pulled the hand mic out of his hand and put it up to my ear, "Bravo three six, this is Bravo six, come in over!" My heart leapt for joy, "Bravo six this is bravo three six, request fire mission polar over." "...six this is bravo six, come in over!" He couldn't hear me, we had one way communication and he was just calling for me over and over. I tossed the mic down and looked at SGT Coca my FO. "Head all the way back up to the trucks, get that radio on the power source and call in a fire mission on this spot, we'll keep moving and meet up with you." Coca nodded and headed back.

"Where's that fucking fire support?!" Johnny yelled in between firing. "I'm fucking trying!" I yelled back right as I saw one of those notorious pizza hats crest the hill to my left on the flank of one of my fire teams that was online. He was perfectly poised to lay down a line of fire hitting every one of them. Immediately I raised my weapon reflexively and shot two rounds that hit the rocks right in front of him. I still remember the frustration as I aimed closer, placing the red dot center mass and pulled the trigger again and again as the guy started running. I could see my rounds hit the rocks in front of him and get closer to hitting him as he ran. I was leading him and raising my point of aim until he darted below the mountain. Whether he fell from my bullets, or just ducked behind cover, I'll never know.

I went back to the low ready and heard the call, "MEDIC!" I leaned forward to see what happened when two bullets whizzed right next to my face coming from different directions. It was almost a reflex as my body dropped backwards onto the ground. I emptied a magazine into a bush in front of me where I thought one of the rounds had come from. The fire to my right intensified as dirt was flying up on the ground next to me. I changed magazines quickly and fired with my left hand emptying another magazine into a bush to my right. I changed magazines again and waited two seconds. No rounds came my direction and I hopped back up to my feet.

"Who is it? What's going on?" I yelled in the direction of the call for medic. "It's Smith, he's ambulatory!" "Alright, keep moving and send him back here." I stood in the middle between both fire teams as I saw Ted Smith dart across in front of me. I couldn't see any injuries on his left side, and he looked to be moving well. I glanced once again to my flank to make sure I didn't see anyone maneuvering from those same bushes that almost ended me, and when I saw it was clear, I continued to move as well.

At one point during the chaos, I looked over at PFC Smith who was a 203 gunner. He was firing his weapon and 203 and every time, I saw blood squirt out whenever he fired a grenade. I assumed he had been hit in the arm, then he pushed up on his front hands to move with the team and I saw what looked like a faucet pouring blood out of his cheek. He was heading in my direction and I could see the entire right side of his face was bloody and swollen. His eye was nearly shut and his skin was turning pale. I must have looked worried when I made eye contact with him because he made it a point to smile with the good half of his face.

SGT Harrell, PFC Smith, and SPC Kirkland after the firefight

When his team got to me, I yelled at his team leader to get Smith back to the trucks, he passed by my side and said, "Smith refuses to leave without his team," and took up a firing position next to me. I grabbed Smith by the IBA as he got closer, "head back to the trucks now!" "Not without my guys sir," this private was openly disobeying me and I couldn't help but respect him for it. "Keep moving Ted, we're right behind you."

I looked up as SGT Zimmerman arrived at our position. The team leader was left handed and for some reason was carrying the SAW. I looked at him and at McKenna who just shook his head. Zimmerman stood up and looked at all of us, "Go! NOW! I'LL COVER YOU!" The young stocky blonde stood up and held the SAW like Rambo pulling on the trigger and laying down a wall of gunfire as the rest of us moved quickly along the path. I could see the brass being ejected bounce off of his bicep as I realized that lefties have even more to deal with when they're in the army. One particular piece of brass stuck to his arm and burned a 5.56 shell casing into his bicep. I thought it went pretty well with his tribal tattoos.

When we arrived at the trucks, we found a couple cases of unopened 203 rounds and started pounding the side of the mountain to cover our escape. At the same time Coca was calling in an ACE report. He told me that A-10's were enroute and I looked around at the team. Zimmerman's SAW had a magazine in it, I was down to one magazine with just tracers and pretty much everyone else was also out of ammo. Smith was starting to get woozy, but wouldn't admit it, and everyone was still out of breath. I called in and after what seemed like hours, I finally talked to my company commander again. Although they started moving when we called in the TIC, he was still more than an hour away. We were still getting pot-shots, but neither us, nor the A-10's could spot the enemy forces. Basically, if they were regrouping for another attack, I didn't have the ammunition to fight back and I made the call to leave the mountain and live to fight another day.

That was more than 10 years ago, and I probably still question that decision at least once every few months. I've gone over a million different ways to deal with it, but it can't be changed. What I took away from that day, however, is how all my guys acted when they were outnumbered, surrounded, physically exhausted, and out of ammunition. Those are the bravest men I've ever seen, they were truly incredible!

CONUS Present Day

You're going into the world of the modern man, if you haven't read the article yet, the New York Times wrote this dribble about 27 ways to be a modern man. I wanted to gouge my eyes out reading it. Apparently the modern man cares about women's shoe sizes, makes sure everyone's electronics are charging, wears Kenneth Cole oxfords and isn't some "gauche simpleton." He owns a melon baller, a shoehorn, and hardwood flooring. He is sometimes the little spoon, cries often, and doesn't have a use for a gun. I don't even know what the fuck a "melon baller" is. I'm a real man, I own a gun and I carry it often, and if you threaten me or mine I will put a controlled pair center mass faster than you can say "gauche simpleton". A real man can kick the modern man's ass, but the real man doesn't hit girls.

I think it's the way people in the real world are afraid to confront threats that I just don't get. Everything and everyone is so soft. We get classes and lessons upon lessons on how to not offend people.   It really pisses me off that it's apparently my responsibility to guard against someone else's weak emotional response to something that challenges their worldview. Get over it, stop being such a wimp. It seems to me that the more the world moves toward this coddling mentality from cradle to grave, the more cynical and angry I get, and the more I want to be offensive. But I can't.

I've said it over and over in this book, and I will say it some more, we have to learn to survive in this world. Unlike us, the civilians don't know the offensive world that exists out there. They simply can't fathom that little boys are raped by their family members and that somehow that's accepted. They can't imagine a place where daughters die accidentally, but if dad gets a couple hundred bucks, it's forgotten and he sleeps just fine that night. It's impossible for them to imagine someone putting a bomb in a church and blowing everyone up inside because they were from a different sect. They can't possibly comprehend what it is to stand over the bloody corpse of your opponent, looking into his empty eyes, thankful that on that day, you were better. The world is ugly, brutal, and evil. We have seen it with our own eyes, tasted the blood, smelled death, and felt the heartbreak of losing someone we loved.

When I tell you it's hard not to have a chip on your shoulder, I mean it. I wake up and thank God for this day. I thank Him to be in a home, with a full belly, taking a hot shower. I thank Him for my wife, my kids, and my job. I thank Him for snatching me from the clutches of death that I might experience the beauty that this world has to offer. Then I ask Him to grant me patience. I ask for patience with those that I work with. I ask him to help me to understand them because they will never understand me, and if I can't understand that I can at least fake it well enough to get through the day.

I had a welder tell me once that I didn't understand how hot it was under that cape. I actually laughed out loud, which was a mistake, but come on! I've been in an Australian APC in southern Iraqi deserts in 140 degrees. I remember when they dropped the tailgate I couldn't wait to step outside to "cool down." Even the Iraqi interpreter looked like he was going to go down with heat exhaustion.

My mistake with this welder was lacking empathy, and this is another common theme throughout the book. Sometimes, actually most times, it's hard to feel empathy. I don't empathize with weakness, I abhor it. Your bitching and whining is only turning me off more, do you have any idea what I've seen and done? No...no they don't. This is something I'm still working on, and most days I find myself going through the motions rather than actually feeling anything, but it's important to stay connected to the people around me. I have to work to put myself in the mind of the person I'm talking to and think about the situation like they are. I ask myself a few questions:

1. How do they feel about this situation?
2. Why do they feel this way?
3. Why are they telling you?
4. What can you do to help?

We may be hard, calculated, and ruthless, but we did all of those things to protect the ones we loved. We stepped in between them and evil, and now that battle is over for us, now we must return to the world that doesn't know evil. Now we must continue to help, and show the world we care, but in a different way, we need to do it in the way that they understand. You want to conform to this world because it's the world that the people you love live in. The very reason I did all that insane stuff was to protect this world, even though I don't understand it some days.

Firefights are sometimes easier than living in a world that doesn't understand us. When we are in combat, we can execute a battle drill that we have done a million times in training. Every man knows his role, and we are confident that our buddy has our backs. We may not know everything about this particular location and enemy, but we know how to find cover, what a good firing position looks like, what support to call in and how to call it. We know our capabilities, strengths, and weaknesses. We have rehearsed over and over, and when we combine this knowledge, experience and practice, we form the greatest warfighting unit mankind has ever known.

That's in battle, but we're not in battle anymore, at least not the kind we've trained for. You have no experience in this world, no support, no training, no preparation, and we wonder why guys struggle at home. Take the lessons learned here and start to apply them. When you're mentally strong, rehearse some of these drills and try them out. As you begin to see success, success will come easier and more naturally. Give yourself a break and a chance to learn, this is not easy and you can't expect it to go perfectly. Keep working at it and don't give up, you can do this and do it well. Give yourself some time and practice...it will come.

7. Risk

Afghanistan 2005

We arrived at the border checkpoint after around 16 hours of driving from FOB Salerno. The checkpoint consisted of triple strand concertina wire strung around a hillside. Near the center was a mortar firing point, and I could see some rucks laid near a tarp by the one building that stood there. I asked the platoon leader that I was replacing where I should drop my stuff. Pete Vanjgel pointed towards the tarp, "Drop your bags there." I nodded and asked where we were sleeping. He smiled and chuckled, "right there," pointing towards the tarp. It was a single piece of angle iron hammered into the ground and four blue, raggedy tarps tied to it. The tarps were stretched out, ripped, and had holes all over them. It looked like a place that provided mediocre shade and probably no cover from the rain. I was not excited to be spending two weeks a month sleeping under there.

Pete spent some time debriefing me on the location with a map on the warm hood of my HMMWV. He showed me some of the common routes the enemy used, and where some of the patrols had been effective. He also made sure to emphasize the threat of indirect fire, predominantly rockets. Although our regular patrolling pretty much kept the enemy from using mortars, the surrounding elevation meant that they could still be very accurate at the max range of their rockets. As Pete got in his truck to leave, I felt a bubbling in my stomach. "Hey, where's the shitter," I asked. "You passed it on the way in, just outside the wire."

His convoy pulled out and silence filled the canyon. The boys had cleared out the trucks and were getting ready to lie down after the long drive. I grabbed a handful of MRE wipes, which we all know are a miserable solution to wiping your ass, and strolled outside the wire to find the designated toilet. I walked about 50 meters outside of the gate and followed my nose to the right spot. Behind a clump of trees, next to a wadi by the wire, was a huge hole. This thing was probably six to eight feet wide and maybe ten feet long, plus another ten feet deep. Laid across the center of this massive canyon was a single 2x6 board. I immediately thought that this was not worth the risk, and I should find another spot, but I didn't have my e-tool, and my stomach was informing me that there was no time to find another location.

They tell you that Ranger school prepares you to handle the rigors of combat both physically and emotionally. I never thought that the log walk from Darby would come into play in Afghanistan, but instead of falling 30 feet into a clean river, I would be falling 10 feet into a rocky shit covered hole. I had an image at this moment of falling and breaking my neck and my soldiers would argue about who would have to fish out my body. I had no real time to assess alternate routes and locations, I was going to drop this deuce, either in this hole or I'd be wearing it for a week.

I stepped out onto the precarious plank, my mind was so focused that the bubble guts even stopped temporarily. I shimmied slowly, one foot in front of the other, never really lifting my feet off of the board. My arms were outstretched completely and I kept an eye on the far side of the board. If it lifted too far off the ground, or shifted to one side, or worse, flipped, I was going tooth first into the rocks below. After about three feet, I decided that I had traveled far enough, and slowly began to lower myself into a sitting position. My feet were dangling in front of me, and I had unbuckled my pants, but now I had to figure out a way to expose my ass without leaning too far forward. There was nothing holding this board, so if the center of balance shifted, I would easily flip this thing upside down. I started to hop in place and inch by inch pull my pants down until I passed my thigh and could put them down over my knees. I looked towards the sky, keeping my center of balance as closely over the board as I could and finally relieved myself.

As my whole body lurched, I thought about the decisions I had made in my life to get me to this position. I thought about all the cool training I had done, and compared this moment to my expectations of entering battle representing my country. Then it occurred to me that I was outside the wire, and if someone decided to attack at this particular moment, there was little I could do without getting covered in human excrement. Then I remembered the toilet paper I had was in my front pants pocket…all the way down by my ankle.

I managed to pull some magnificent Chinese contortionist move to get my hand into my pants pocket and pull out my wipes.

Without missing a beat, I cleaned myself and caught my breath. I now had a decision to make: I could either try and pull my pants up on this board without falling, or I could risk a splinter in my balls and shimmy to the safe edge. I examined the board closely, running my hand along it sideways, assessing the risk of splinters. I decided that I would rather pull a splinter out of my sack than someone else's turd out of my teeth and began to slide.

I gritted my teeth in painful anticipation as I felt the cool wood slide below me. When I made the trip safely, I laid down in the dirt and pulled my pants up and laughed as I stared up at the Afghan night sky. I had made it, and look at all those stars!

I mentioned in the introduction that I have been promoted a couple times and I'm currently a program manager. A program manager is the person that leads the process from a great idea to a product in the hands of the consumer. The process of identifying a customer need, identifying solutions for that need, and implementing those solutions, particularly in a manufactured instead of a digital product, usually takes several years and several million dollars. I made a name for myself in Iowa for leading a team to do a new product in 8 months for about $250,000. It was a simple project, but unheard of at the time.

Today I'm working on a much more complicated product with many more regulatory and emissions regulations that has low volumes. It's often tough to have a great return on investment on Low volume projects, but we still pursue them because they are necessary for the business and the right thing to do for the customer. Our team and leadership is extremely risk averse, they literally suffer from analysis paralysis. I heard about this in the

Army, but I never really saw it until now that I'm in the corporate world. Gentlemen, I'm working on a project that has been in limbo for three years! They have spent three years researching options and going back to the drawing board without actually doing the program!

You know the saying, "A good decision now is better than a great decision later." We're about to learn that lesson the hard way. Regulatory requirements have created a drop dead date for our product and now we have less than a year to come up with a solution. People are scrambling, and I've been bringing them together to make decisions. Over the last week, we've spent around six hours in meeting rooms discussing different options and I felt like we had a good idea with a couple recommendations that had different levels of risk.

This morning the lead design engineer came up to me and said he was uncomfortable with one of the options because he didn't have the full picture yet. I about flipped my desk. This guy won't take a step until he has researched and analyzed every possible circumstance that can occur, and if you try and move him forward, he's going to keep telling everyone that he's uncomfortable because he doesn't know what the next step may bring. Here's the thing, we have about 90% of the information, and the stuff that we don't know, even in their worst case, won't significantly impact the schedule or budget of the program!

I have found that this is in large part a cultural issue. Somehow these people get promoted to positions where they can significantly impact the direction of the business, and we need to learn how to maneuver around them. I don't mean, go behind their backs, I mean learn how to guide them to a decision. You're not in a position to make people execute on your unilateral decision, and at least how my company is organized, very few people are. Collaboration and buy-in is key, and in many circumstances, far too many, it creates a world of extremely slow decision making.

Survival Tip: If you want to encourage cultural change, take it in baby steps

Something you're going to have to learn to deal with is a limited amount of decision making authority. "I have to talk to my boss," is a sentence I get tired of hearing, and this goes up so many levels. In my case, however, I'm more likely to hear after the fact, "you need to come talk to me before making those decisions." Very few people lose their jobs for making a good decision now, and one of the reasons military veterans are sought after is their decision making ability.

Imagine if none of your subordinates made decisions without consulting you first. You would be inundated with emails and phone calls and questions and the key decisions that you actually needed to make would get missed because of some silly BS that a subordinate couldn't figure out. This is what is happening in corporate America every day. Some managers have figured out how to disseminate authority while keeping responsibility, but they are few and far between, you may see them at the President level and above. We need to train our subordinates and managers in the workplace to understand this.

Subordinates are much easier to train in this regard. You've done it before, so this shouldn't come as a surprise. You walk them through to a solution, then you tell them to do that themselves in the future. A manager who is unwilling or very apprehensive to disseminate authority is much more difficult to train.

1. Start by assessing their comfort level in decision making authority. When you've been counseled more than once, then you've figured out where that comfort level is
2. Don't present the decision as something for them to make, rather present it as a decision you have already made:
    a. I'm doing XXXX, any issues with that?
    b. Don't say- should I do XXXX or YYYY? Even if you have been told several times that you don't have the authority to make a decision, if you don't present a solution, that authority will never be given to you
3. As you develop rapport, then request authority to make that decision in the future

You will find that over time, even the most apprehensive managers will start giving you more and more authority, and you will be more satisfied at work. If you train your peers to do this as well, you will find that the culture in your workplace will start to change slowly. All of this is good for your sanity, and good for the business.

They hired you above someone else because you are willing and able to make decisions, and when they think of the future of their company, they see it in the hands of someone like you.

8. Razzle Dazzle

Afghanistan 2005

Because of the remote location of Camp Tillman, we had a special waiver where we only had to turn in our local cash quarterly instead of monthly. Basically, for those of you that don't know, the Army gives you cash to pay locals to do work for you on your base. In our case we used it for water trucks, janitor type stuff, trash disposal, and any other emergencies where we needed to buy from the local economy. I was in charge of the cash and I had a small safe for it, and Pete Vanjgel was in charge of deciding where the money was spent. We each kept receipts, and once every few months, we had to catch a ring-route helicopter flight back to the main FOB to square our funds and get new money. I regularly traveled with about $10,000 of Afghani cash, which looked like a hundred billion dollars and weighed like 80 lbs.

Anyway, we caught the flight back and our goal was to turn in our cash, get the new money, and catch a new flight in a couple days. I was coming back from a mission and just as I crossed the wire at Camp Tillman, I saw the incoming flight, he was early and I therefore was in a rush. I ran to the safe, picked up my dough, threw my three day bag on and met up with Pete on the flight line. When we arrived at the FOB, several hours later, we finally had a chance to check our books. It seemed that we were off, I can't remember exactly how much money we were off, but it wasn't much, less than $50. We all know how the finance guys are in the army though, so with this error, there was no way we'd be getting on a flight in two days. We counted and recounted and recounted again, there was no way of making it work, so we hatched up a plan. We called it Razzle Dazzle.

Pete is a pretty guy, and I mean that objectively. He was an introvert and kind of an asshole, but chicks loved him. I'm not going into the details of what he looked like because there's really no way of doing it without sounding super gay. Dark hair, light eyes, Men's Health model body... there. Anyway, I on the other hand am very much an extrovert with a great sense of humor and not nearly as pretty. We decided that as soon as we walked in, we would find a young lady in the room. Pete would distract her with his good looks, and I would fire off jokes and compliments to keep her laughing and unfocused. This would continue until we got the stamp and our papers were put away. I was Razzle, he was Dazzle.

We walked into the small wooden office and both picked the same target immediately upon entering. I reached deep into the memories of 80's movies and channeled my best Eddie Murphy as Axel Foley in Beverly Hills Cop and became a huge distraction. The entire office was looking our way and laughing within seconds. Our target was smiling ear to ear and waved us over. I honestly don't remember what I said at all but somehow we were laughing so hard that I was wiping tears out of my eyes.

Every time she looked up from the papers and locked eyes with Pete, her cheeks turned bright red and she quickly looked back down at her paper. We got our stamp and walked out of there like we just won the super bowl laughing and high-fiving each other all the way back to our hooch.

It turned out that we could have just fessed up about the fifty bucks and gone through the days of paperwork because our return home flight got cancelled and the two of us got stuck on this base while our company was out running missions in a completely different part of Afghanistan. We spent the next week as full blown fobbits, hitting the gym several times a day, eating hot chow every meal, and working on our Madden '05 characters. To this day, I still can't hear half of the songs on that soundtrack without going back to that week on FOB Salerno.

Halloween was interesting this year. The factory manager sent out a note telling people that they could wear a costume on the Friday of Halloween weekend. I chuckled to myself, but I really didn't expect to see anything. Boy was I wrong! There were all kinds of costumes running around, and I tried to take a picture of every one. At first I thought it was ridiculous, and then later I realized, it's still ridiculous, but at least they were having fun.

I watched as these people came strolling in for the day and logged into their computers as if it was any other normal day. Whoa, whoa, whoa, don't try and act like you're not dressed up in some ridiculous looking outfit right now! One guy dressed like an Elmer's glue bottle came to talk to me about one of the programs that I'm running. He had an Elmer's t-shirt and a bright orange beanie with a white tip. We started by having a serious work conversation and my eyes kept drifting towards the beanie. I was thinking that it was a particularly clever outfit, but I wondered where he found that shirt. Someone at some point made a shirt with an Elmer's glue logo on it, and put it on the shelf. This guy saw it and exchanged money for it, and based on the way that it was faded, he's owned this shirt for a while. Now that beanie, it looks like he put a hole in the top of it, which would make sense, I mean, where are you going to find a bright orange beanie with a white ball on top. Wait, is he wearing a santa hat underneath? That must be hot to wear all that, I'd definitely be sweating.

I recognized the pause in conversation, my eyes locked with his and I realized that he had been talking to me about something important. I laughed, "sorry dude, I missed all of that. I'm just," I motioned to his outfit with my hand. He laughed as well and posed like a bottle of glue. After two or three more tries, he finally got through his whole thought and we took care of it. That was a really unproductive conversation now that I think of it.

There was another Indian fellow that made me break into hard laughter, and he wasn't even talking to me. Early that morning there was a costume parade, I shit you not, there was a parade in the office. Everyone that was in costume started strolling around the cubicles in character giving people a laugh. It was all in good fun, but they didn't spend much time in my area. I smiled and they moved on. As they came back around later, they made a stop at the cubicle next to mine to harass the lady that works there. This guy walked up to her and asked, "Do you know what I'm dressed up as?"

"A baseball player," she answered inquisitively.

"Yes, but what kind of baseball player," his Punjab accent was strong but his words were clear.

"A player from Cleveland right?"

"Yes, and what are the players from Cleveland?"

"Indians."

"Right. You get it? I'm a Cleveland Indi..."

Before he was done with the sentence I burst out into laughter, maybe to the point of bordering inappropriate, but it's his racial joke, I'm just laughing at it. He turned and gave me a thumbs up as others slowly started to get the joke as well. I still haven't gotten a chance to get to know that guy, but I'm convinced he's awesome.

The point is that sometimes life is ridiculous, whether it's in the army or in the civilian world, and we really can't take it too seriously. Yeah, the costumes might be stupid, but it's fun for them, so take a minute and enjoy it with them. Don't be a pretentious prick with a chip on your shoulder incapable of having a good time. CSM Plumley was a badass, and he was portrayed amazingly in "We Were Soldiers", but being that angry all the time in the civilian world is not going to get you anywhere. I can't even imagine how he would have reacted if he were in my office that day.

So take a step back and relax, laugh at something stupid, and let people have fun. You know how short life can be, enjoy it because someday soon it's going to be over for all of us. We have plenty of reasons to be sad and angry, look for an excuse to be happy and laugh. Let it come, don't fight it, and don't be afraid to let your guard down.

9. Expectations

Just yesterday I was having a Facebook discussion with a friend about troop pay. One of the comments on the thread was as follows: "I'm a SSG with several deployments, multiple awards, and I only make $55k a year." That one line prompted me to write this chapter because I've seen this come up several times among my peers. You might be valuable as a soldier, but what do you know about running a business?

If you are going to continue working for the government, then your experience matters and you may actually see a bump in pay by getting out. If, like me, you are completely disillusioned with government and don't want to work for them again, then you are starting at the bottom. I'm sorry, it's just the way it is, there's a benefit which I'll explain in a minute, but you have to start at the bottom. I'd say the chances of that SSG getting out and immediately making $55,000 a year right off the bat are pretty small, especially if he doesn't have a degree in engineering or supply chain management.

I don't care if you are a retiring Lieutenant Colonel, you probably don't know anything about SAP or material presentation and flow. You probably know very little about labor laws or how to improve productivity and efficiency on a manufacturing floor. It's unlikely you can identify poor welds or their root cause. You probably don't know what it means when you're told that we have to implement a touch for quality to reduce low-hour warranty. Get where I'm going here? There's a lot to learn about the business, and you can't hop right into a management position until you understand that.

Most of the soldiers I know that have degrees get them in general business, some sort of "leadership", or criminal justice. These really aren't the most valuable degrees, and there are better ways to make that investment. If you are planning on a degree right now, don't spend your time and money on something without a practical application. Stick to things like accounting, engineering (electrical, mechanical or industrial to a lesser extent), supply chain management, and maybe marketing. I have a degree in history which has only served to hinder my opportunities, luckily I'm an expert bullshitter and have found ways to equate some utility in my degree to whichever job I'm applying for, but if I can keep you from making the same mistake, I will.

Also just as valuable as a degree are certifications. These you can get with some studying and minimal investment on your part. Think about what career you want to go into, for Program Management which is what I do, there's a PMP certification that carries a ton of weight. It's a long application process, but the test is four hours and that's it, I have a credential just as valuable as my MBA which took me almost two years to earn.

If you can afford to get an advanced degree, I strongly recommend that. Look for a Master's or even a Doctorate. I still haven't gotten a PhD, and I'm not entirely certain that I will, but I have seen people get hired and interviewed above others with experience just because they have that degree. So if you're a shy person, or you don't interview well, then you're going to want to take a serious look at getting that post-baccalaureate degree.

The civilian doesn't care about your awards and likely doesn't understand them either. You should avoid over-emphasizing any valor awards you received, except putting them on your resume. Don't talk about them in your interview, save those stories for social situations around some beers. People are easily intimidated, and if they know they are working next to a real-life badass, they are more likely to avoid you or be extra sensitive to everything you say.

So your experience doesn't mean anything, your awards are worthless and in some cases can intimidate people, and you wasted your time and money on your degree, what the hell?

The skills you have that set you apart from the competition are not things you put on a resume. These may seem simple, but they are what set you apart from the average civilian or recent college graduate:

- You will show up to work on time if not early, every single day.
- You will not call in sick on a whim, rarely if ever pulling that card.
- You will work hard when you are at work.
- You will make decisions and stand by them.
- You will show honesty and integrity because you are not a coward.

- You will show everyone respect, and it will take you years to get used to calling people by their first names.
- You will not be afraid to give bad news, and you will do so quickly to help find a solution.
- You are an excellent planner, and when something goes wrong, your first thought is "how do we fix this" not "who do I blame for this."

These skills are what set you apart from millions upon millions of other job applicants and should be the focus of how you market yourself no matter what occupation you choose.

Don't get it twisted gentlemen, you're not going to walk out of the military as an E8 or O4 and walk into a six figure salary. It's not going to happen. You don't understand the business, you don't know the customer base, you don't have any experience in each different process, so you have to start at or near the bottom. So you have a difficult decision to make. Do you get out into the civilian world, or do you transition into government work?

I've seen guys on both sides of this regret their decision.

If you get out and work for the government, you're still subject to the whims of government. You can end up on different shifts or even deployed again. If there's another fight over the budget in congress, your pay could stop without warning. You also have limited upward mobility, and if you get a crappy boss, you're going to keep that turd for a long time. You do make more money as soon as you get out, and you generally get pretty good benefits, but you're dealing with Tricare still.

If you decide to get out of government work altogether, you're going to make less money to start. You can expect to make as much as your base pay, so take out BAH and COLA and any other allotments you might get and think about how you're going to live on that salary. Because of your skills, however, you're going to get promoted quickly, probably every 18-24 months in the right company. This does require some flexibility on your part, however, and you need to be willing to take the jobs that no one wants, move when it might be inconvenient, and be willing to go where you're needed. You also have the freedom to leave at any point if you feel you are being mistreated. If the need for variable shift work comes up, you get to choose if you want to work a different shift. Also, you will get paid for overtime work, and can always plan your vacations, sometimes even years in advance.

Clearly I have a preference for not working for government, but I leave that decision to you. What I don't want is for you to get out thinking everyone is going to be begging you to come work for them and waving six figures in your face because you deployed a couple times and have a security clearance; they're not. You're going to have to fight into a good job, and when you get there, you're going to have to fight again and again. You're going to have to prove yourself to be an asset and you will. The great news is that your desire for promotion will be the only limiting factor in how high you will go with the company you choose.

9. Expectations

MAJ Schreiner and Me

Part 2
Family Man

10. The Commitment

Arizona 2009

There were three of us going to the Captain's Career Course in Sierra Vista, Arizona who decided that we wanted to live in Tucson 75 miles away. I met Steve at SFAS, we were both squad leaders until I dislocated my knee on the obstacle course and he wasn't selected. We saw each other again while going through PCS at Ft. Bragg; I was going into housing as he was coming out. We met our third, Matt the ginger in the actual Captain's Course. Within the first 10 minutes, we recognized a fellow smartass and the three of us became instant friends.

Those nine months in the career course were insane. We partied far too hard, once even waking up on a Friday morning and deciding to go to Las Vegas that night. We partied in a booth next to Britney Spears, saw Quest crew perform in a club, and wasted far too much money on alcohol. We even stole a full size John Wayne cutout that our course instructor had in his classroom and took it with us to Vegas, getting pictures of The Duke in all sorts of interesting situations.

It was St. Patrick's Day 2009 and my life was about to change drastically. We walked into our favorite bar in Tucson high-fiving the bouncers at The Shanty, grabbed ourselves a table and started telling jokes. The bar filled quickly, as most Irish bars do on St. Patrick's day, and we found ourselves in a great spot to harass people right by the door. As I sipped my drink and talked to my friends, I saw a red flash from the corner of my eye. I turned and looked, there was a cute blonde with short hair walking past our table.

"Who the fuck wears a red shirt on St. Patty's day," I yelled my question at her before she could make her way out the door. She spun around and looked at me, "Who are you talking to?" I quipped back instantly, "Do you see anyone else with a red shirt? It's St. Patty's day," my enthusiasm was palpable. I remember the look she gave me, but I'm not sure exactly what happened next, or how it worked out, yet we managed to get her and her friend to sit at our table.

Emily still says that she can tell I was a dog because we separated her and her friend immediately. She was cute, funny, and had a ton of spunk. She challenged even my best witty comments, and despite her poor fashion sense on this particular holiday, I could tell that she was very smart. A couple months later, right as I was getting ready to PCS to Aberdeen Proving Grounds, I got the text from Emily, "we have to talk."

Steve and I were coming out of the gym when I got the text. My heart sank because I knew it couldn't be good news. Steve kept reassuring me that everything was fine, as a good friend can be expected to, but I knew that something was wrong, I just didn't know what. I pulled into my apartment and grabbed a seat on my couch. I sat and stared at the wall in front of me wondering what it could be, then there was a knock at my door.

Being the strong woman that she is, Emily walked in, sat down and told me she was pregnant. She said she was having the baby, and didn't need my help. Basically I could be as involved as I wanted to be. Then she stood up and walked out, leaving me sitting on my couch contemplating everything she just dropped on me. The entire conversation lasted no more than five or ten minutes. Emily still jokes about how she wished she had a camera that day to capture the look of sheer terror on my face. I'm proud to say, six years later and she still hasn't seen it repeated.

I had a lot of soul searching to do, and a 2,000 mile drive to think about it. My stuff was packed into containers as I filled my little Honda with necessities and started the drive from Tucson to Aberdeen, Maryland. As much as I tried, I couldn't shake off the idea that my life would never be the same. Being a dad had been thrust upon me and I really wasn't ready for it.

My child didn't ask to come into this world. He didn't make any irresponsible choices. He was blameless, and I could either make the decision to be a father, or I could skirt my responsibilities and be a dirt bag. The latter is the move of a coward, someone who is unwilling to accept consequences, afraid of a little discomfort, and I've said it before, I'm not a coward.

By the time I got to Maryland, I had decided unequivocally, that I was going to make a commitment to that child. I was going to be a father, a loving father, a positive and regular influence in my child's life. Here is the greatest revelation I made on that drive:

I was done living my life for myself.

That's the first step in becoming a parent. When you realize that someone else's life matters more to you than your own, every decision you make now hinges on the benefit that decision has for someone other than yourself. Although I had intellectually accepted that, it still took me some time to start living my life that way. I couldn't spend money without thinking of someone else, I couldn't come home and plop myself in front of the couch, I couldn't just leave the dishes for tomorrow. All of these things took time to realize and to start living like a father.

I still wanted to do all the hooah things that I could in the Army and almost ended up in a secret squirrel job that would have kept me away from home about 75% of the time. I went through the entire application process and ended up in a non-descript building somewhere near the capital for a week long round of interviews. As I sat in these people's offices, I noticed a lot of pictures of kids, but not so many pictures of husbands and wives. I realized that my young marriage couldn't really handle the stress of living in some third world country and me being gone all the time. Instead, I decided to get out altogether, look for that 9-5 job, and give up on adrenaline rushes.

North Carolina 2015

Just recently I had a dream that I was back in the Army. I met up with a group of soldiers during a mission brief. We got bussed over to green ramp and got our parachutes to jump. I remember being excited to be surrounded by hardened soldiers, jumping into a training event. I felt the cool rush of air as my chute opened up and I could see the lights on the DZ in the darkness. We formed up and did a forced march to a firing range. When we got there we did some firing and room clearing and headed back to the company HQ. It was amazing and I was having so much fun.

When we got the headquarters our deployment gear was packed, and my family was standing at the edge of the parking lot. My wife was crying and my daughter came running to my arms. She held to me tightly and cried uncontrollably. I didn't want to let go and her words stung, "I don't want you to go daddy." I felt a knot in my throat and turned to look at one of the soldiers. I looked at him and said, "I don't want to miss a year of their lives." "You don't have to; you're not in the Army anymore."

My eyes flew open and I examined the darkness of my room. I was back in the same house I lived in as a Lieutenant in the 82nd, and being back near Bragg had clearly caused this dream. The fan whirred overhead and beads of sweat pooled on my face. I wiped my face in the darkness and looked around the room, reassuring myself that I was in a different time and place from my very real dream. I glanced down to my right and saw, with the aid of blue moonlight creeping in the room, my wife sleeping peacefully next to me.

I got up out of bed, walked down the hallway and quietly opened the door to my two older kids' room. I couldn't see the boy in the top bunk, but his sister was sprawled out on the bottom bunk. She was no longer covered and she was drooling out of a wide open mouth. The nightlight lit up her bright pink strawberry shortcake jammies. She had pushed the covers almost completely off the bed and only had one pillow left. I almost laughed as I moved her back onto her pillow and covered her up. When I kissed her forehead, she put her hand on my face and the slightest of smiles began to form on her mouth before it dropped open again and she began to snore.

I really miss the Army some days. I miss the excitement, training soldiers, and my brothers. Some of you know from first-hand experience, however, what it's like to say goodbye to your babies. That's a pain that I simply don't want. I have willingly given up all the best parts of the Army so that I can get greeted by three excited little minions every single day. I made a commitment to them, really to their older brother, that I would be there and live my life for him. It was a promise only I could hear, and until now, I've never told anyone. I am a man of my word.

If you haven't already made a commitment to your children, do so now. Don't wait until you have everything else fixed in your life, don't wait until your marriage is better, don't wait until your finances are more stable, don't wait until you've got your own head straight. Do it now. Time is not on your side, and they don't care about anything except whether or not you are there. Just be there and do things with them. Whatever it is that they like to do, share it with them.

Survival Tip: Make time every single day to spend with your kids.

For many of us, the most joyful memories we have of our youth are from moments we shared with our parents. I think of George Straight's song "The Best Day" when the little boy gets so excited about camping with his dad that it's the best day of his life. There's a lot of truth to that song and that sentiment. For a little boy, hanging out with him is the best gift a dad can give. Be there for your kids, and have your mind on them and what you're doing with them, don't be staring at your phone.

My kids know that they are a priority in my life, and from the moment I walk in the door after work, until they are in bed, I'm there for them. Some days it's really difficult, they often try my patience, and occasionally I lose it, but I'm there. I don't have it all together, and I can't always get them what they want, but they know who their daddy is and they know he loves them. My children bring me immeasurable joy, and I will never regret my choice to commit my life to them and their mother.

Gentlemen, on our final day, we aren't going to ask people to bring us our cars, or our golf clubs, we're not going to be concerned about how our favorite sports team is faring. We're going to want to see our children, they are the legacy we will leave in this world and we will live on in their memories. What do you want your legacy to be?

11. Patience

Afghanistan 2005

We had been on the hilltop for several days. The weather had taken a turn for the worse and rain and hail came down hard. When we scaled the mountain we only brought three day packs with us, and after running out of ammunition in a different firefight, most of us used our packs for additional rounds. I had my woobie and two MRE's plus my camelback. Besides that there were several magazines, a couple smoke grenades, and some 203 rounds just in case.

We had spent the last couple days on our stomachs. CPT Teague decided to pull all the troops back and leave us on the mountain top as bait. The idea was to see if we could get the

SGT Zimmerman, SGT Harrell, Me, SPC McHugh, SGT Coca, SPC Hobbs, CPT Teague, PFC Mignone, SPC Kirkland

enemy to attack thinking that there was a much smaller force on the mountain, then bring the whole company in behind as support. Although it was just my platoon up there, we wanted to look as small as possible, plus none of us really wanted to get pegged by a sniper.

My medic and I built a small hooch with both of our woobies and pine needles. It was just wide and tall enough for both of us to fit. Yes, I definitely used another man for heat, and if you want to criticize, then you've never been really cold and wet. Each day we took a few minutes to improve our shelter, adding camouflage and cover, but we were quickly running out of food and water. I was cold, wet, hungry, and tired and I really didn't think the attack was ever going to come. Several of my guys were joking about when they were going to get their Ranger tabs.

We had a few guys with us with some SIGINT capabilities and were intercepting enemy communications. One of the guys had worked for the history channel back when it did actual history shows, and we spent a lot of time asking him about that. We were chatting one day, after smoking the last of our cigarettes when the interpreter put his finger up to quiet us. Unlike normal terps, this guy was an American citizen with a top secret clearance and an awesome attitude. He focused clearly on his headset and looked up, "the attack is coming tonight." Our JTAC got on the horn and started looking for assets that we could pull to help us during the fight that was coming.

If I told you that this was the week of June 25th, 2005, some of you will quickly know what was going on at that time in Afghanistan. Marcus Luttrell, the Navy SEAL who wrote the book "Lone Survivor" had gotten into a firefight with his team, and pretty much every single air asset had been diverted to support that mission. On the ground though, we had no idea. All I knew was that we had been on that mountaintop several days and no air asset in country was unavailable. Our JTAC was doing the best he could, arguing about what it meant to be Troops In Contact, but he lost. All I remember was him looking at us and saying that there was another big TIC somewhere to the north and everyone was going there. Even after several days on that mountaintop, we still couldn't get support. I was angry and I felt like a sitting duck. It wasn't until a few weeks later that I would learn why I couldn't get help that day, and then I felt like an asshole. Sorry Marcus.

So we prepared ourselves for the onslaught. We beefed up our firing positions as much as possible, and made sure that we had TRP's established. I passed out the extra ammunition I was carrying and put magazines in easy to reach places in firing positions. Our gear was inspected, and we waited as a dense fog began to fill the mountaintop. Our visibility slowly got worse and worse, it was like a ring surrounding the hilltop. I could see surrounding hills clearly, but all our fields of fire were clouded.

The interpreter came to find me, "looks like they're making final preparations, they are about to come. There are a lot of them. Did you get any air support?" I could tell he was worried, these were intel guys and they were stuck on this mountaintop too. They were not trained infantry paratroopers, but they were handling themselves really well. "No, we're on our own tonight, but we have mortars and the boys are ready," I responded. He nodded, but I could tell he was apprehensive. "They're praying, this is it," he looked at me again and his eyes were asking me to do something.

11. Patience

I've seen fear in men's eyes, and I'm not sure exactly what he was hearing on that radio, but this guy was legitimately concerned about what was coming our way. I knew that we didn't have any air assets, we really couldn't see anything directly in front of us, and ground troops were a minimum 30-40 minutes away, which in a firefight is an eternity. From my position on the mountain, I could see in the distance a blazing fire with the shadows of men huddled around it.

I called in what I saw and asked if I could get clearance to fire high explosives at them, the problem was that they were in Pakistan (we were right on the border). I couldn't get clearance for HE, but I was told that I could use Illumination rounds. I was pissed, and completely out of patience. I couldn't get air support, the 105 artillery was out of range, and I couldn't fire 120 mortar HE rounds. Basically I wasn't going to get any help until my position was overrun. So I made a creative choice.

I crawled to the edge of the ridgeline with the Viper, which for those of you who don't know is a set of binoculars with two buttons on it. When you click one button you will get a distance and the other you get a direction, with a GPS for your grid, you have an instant polar fire mission. The problem was that the heavy fog was disrupting the Viper and I was getting the wrong readings. It was time to use my IOBC/Ranger School skills yet again.

I pulled out a paper map and compass and fired an azimuth at the target. I then calculated the range based on their location on the terrain using the map, finally I did a little extra math and figured out an elevation for the Illumination round. "Bravo six, this is bravo three six, fire mission polar over," I called in the fire mission giving my distance, direction, elevation, and requested the illumination round. The distinct voice of the mortar sergeant came on the line, "Check elevation over." I immediately fired back, "the elevation is right over." There was a long pause then a squelch, "roger standby." I could hear him chuckle briefly and if you could tell someone is smiling over the radio, this was it.

"Shot over." I heard the round fire and stared through the binoculars intently at the fire. My FO was lying next to me with a giant grin on his face as well. BOOM! The round impacted directly on the fire sending flames flying in all directions and then it exploded too. Trees caught fire and I saw mass chaos in the area. The shadows were running this way and that, and I could tell they were dragging people. The terp piped up, "the prayer stopped midsentence." I laughed, yeah, I just hit them with an illumination round. It was a one in a billion shot, so of course I got on the radio, "repeat over." SGT Coca laughed and we high-fived each other... "Shot over."

North Carolina 2015

Your kids will try your patience in ways that you didn't know a fellow human being was capable of. With most people, when they start to piss you off, you can pretty much walk away, not with your kids. When it comes to your kids, you have to sit there and take it, and when they misbehave, it's a reflection on you. For your parents, when you have children, it's like them getting revenge. They are God's little way of teaching us perspective. I remember my mom yelling at me when I was being a smartass teenager, "I hope your kid is as much of a smartass to you, then I'll have my revenge." She could be creative when she was pissed, but what more can you expect from a Cuban mother?

11. Patience

It was Monday night, really this story could happen on any given Monday, but this particular Monday, my oldest son must have been pretty tired. My wife got back from the gym with the kids not long after I got home from work. I met the minivan in the garage and could see her smiling face in the driver seat as the car came to a stop. It's moments like these that I want to take a quick second and thank God for choosing to bless me for some reason because I certainly don't deserve it.

The side door slid open and my daughter called out to me excitedly. I gave her a kiss and as I began to unbuckle my oldest boy who is almost six, he began to cry and whine about something. I say "something" because a) it doesn't really matter what he's crying about and b) there's no way of understanding a five year old when he's got that crying/whining snotty speech going. I pulled my daughter out of the car while he kept yelling. At this point he was kicking his legs and screaming as well. I looked at my wife, "what's his problem?" She had the baby in one hand and shook her head and shrugged her shoulders as she grabbed our girl by the hand and started to walk inside. I leaned forward to his car seat in the middle of the van and unbuckled him as his legs kicked.

"Jonathan, I can't understand you, what's going on?" He continued to throw a fit, so I gave up trying to understand. I finished getting him out of his car seat and helped him get into the house where his fit continued. Now that he was out of his seat, he decided to literally run circles around the house flapping his arms, screaming and crying as he did. At this point I was starting to get angry. I don't do well when people whisper or whine, and tears in general do not illicit empathy from me. If I see an adult crying, someone better be dead, when my kids cry,

I'm learning to feel differently, but it still depends on the mood I'm in. This is something I acknowledge that I need to work on. He's a little boy, a five year old boy, and whatever is going on is the most important thing in his little world. He doesn't have the perspective that I do on life and he doesn't understand that there are kids out there that will risk getting hit by a truck for a bottle of water.

I told him once again that he needed to calm down, this time more forcefully and I started to raise my voice. "OK! FINE," he yelled at me, stomped on the ground and started running around the kitchen, throwing his body against the back door and stomping further. I could feel my blood boil and my wife stepped in. She grabbed his arm and gave him a hug. Let me tell you something gents, a hug was the last thing I was thinking about, but it worked, he calmed down! I stood there in awe of Emily as she got up and kissed him on the forehead. Two seconds later, he was running around playing with his brother and sister as if he hadn't been crying at all.

Moments like these have played out again and again over the years, but I'm so damn stubborn that it still hasn't sunk in for me, and I just keep escalating with my kids instead of calming them down. I expect them to respond when they are scolded, and I hate having to repeat myself. Think about that for a second, I'm expecting a five year old and a three year old to do exactly what I tell them, the first time I tell them, without having to repeat myself. For a guy that's relatively intelligent, I can be a real idiot when it comes to my kids.

A little while later it was dinner time. Jonathan started crying about the food as usual and thus began another fight at the dinner table. He didn't like anything on his plate and made it a point to tell my wife that the food was disgusting. He pushed his plate and placemat across the table, sending his fork and spoon skidding across the wooden table. I looked at him sternly and raised my voice, "Jonathan, put your food in front of you. I don't care if you don't eat, you won't disrespect our dinner time." "OK! FINE," once again, he hopped out of his seat and began running around the kitchen flapping his arms and throwing himself on the floor.

Again I escalated the situation, standing up out of my chair and prepping my knife hand. My wife saw it, put her hand up and walked over to him. "Jonathan, I understand you're having a hard time, but you need to sit at the table with us sweetie." He wiped his tears with his arm, and after a few short breaths, he calmed down and came to sit with us. He pulled his plate close to him as my wife asked him how his day was. "It was fun! We played at PE today," he said as he grabbed some chicken and began to eat. That same chicken that he said was disgusting earlier, now he was eating as though nothing had happened. We made it through the meal, and then it was time to get ready for bath.

I'm not sure what it was about this time, but Jonathan threw yet another tantrum while we got ready for bath, and this time I quickly went into a rage. I stood up and immediately started yelling, his little face turned red, he yelled at the top of his lungs and ran off into his bedroom. I took a deep breath and I was trying to calm myself down when I heard the door slam and I lost it. I stormed towards his room and threw open the door. He was standing behind the door and tried to push it shut. I reached around and grabbed his flailing arms so as not to get hit. I went full knife hand on a five year old boy, yelling at him like a Drill Sergeant would.

At this point my wife came to the rescue once again. The mere sight of her calmed us both down enough for us to talk about what had just happened. Both he and I apologized to each other and he wrapped his little arms tightly around my neck. He then planted his feet and tried to push me to the ground, so I let him and we both fell down into a hug on the carpet floor in his room. He has an infectious giggle once he gets going and we laid there laughing for a couple minutes. I gave him a kiss on the forehead and we started bath time.

I can't expect my five year old to behave any other way than what he did. Some of you are reading this story and thinking that he is a little brat, but he isn't. He's actually a really sweet boy, but on this particular day he was very tired. We had kept them up past bed time the night prior and he had a long day at school, plus my wife had just taken them to a kids Zumba class, so he was exhausted. He was also very hungry because he didn't eat everything provided at lunch, nor during his snack. If you have kids, then you know that the combination of hungry and tired is pretty much asking for this sort of behavior.

The person that should have behaved differently there was me. I really do know better, and I should have done a better job of keeping my cool. For so many years I had grown accustomed to releasing the angry beast, it was in a controlled fashion, but I released him nonetheless. Any perceived threat and the cage was flying open, I didn't react, I over-reacted with such violence of action until the threat was eliminated.

Survival Tip: Your family is not a threat, don't treat them like one

I'm still working on figuring out how to keep my cool when my patience is tested. These are the people that I love the most in this world, why do I have the least amount of patience with them? I think in part because I know they will always be there, or maybe it's because of the amount of time I'm with them. I'm not sure, but I do know that I need to get better at it. My kids are not privates, my wife is not an NCO, my family is not a threat...and neither is your family.

They are the most important people, so we should start treating them that way. We are the sheepdogs who willingly wrote a blank check with our lives on it, ready for it to be cashed for people we don't even know, many of them are assholes. Every day we encounter them in public, and we are cordial and nice, but then when it comes to our dearest, we have so little left over. We need to remind ourselves of how special these people are and focus on being the best version of ourselves for them, not just for the people on the street.

A little over a year ago, I took Jonathan to the store, just the two of us. I promised him that he could get a bumblebee transformer that he had been looking at. The toy he had found was at Target, but I needed some stuff at Walmart, so I took him there instead. Turns out Walmart didn't have the toy that he wanted. I pulled another bumblebee off the shelf and gave it to him. I could see on his face that he really wasn't as excited about it, but we've taught him plenty about receiving gifts. He looked down as he held the toy in his hand and forced a smile. "Thank you Daddy, but we can't buy me something without getting something for Izzy too." He was only four years old at the time, but still

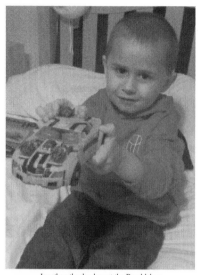
Jonathan the day he got the Bumblebee

showed gratitude for the gift that he didn't want, and not just that, he understood that he couldn't come home without a present for his sister as well. I looked at his little face and felt a knot in my throat, "Put it back, we're going to Target to get the one you wanted."

My wife had specifically told me not to buy that one for the boy, it was more expensive and far too difficult for him, but there was no way I wasn't going to reward that behavior. We walked into target and he took off in a sprint towards the toy section laughing and galloping as he went. He pulled the toy off the shelf and asked me what we should get his sister as he hugged his toy. These are the moments that make parenthood worthwhile. I can't describe the pride and joy I got from this day, and every time I see him transform that toy, I'm reminded of how he earned it even if he isn't.

Do your kids a favor and give them the best of you as much as you can. Work on keeping your cool, even when they test you, and respond with more love. I know it's out of character, but just like anything it takes practice. Make a mental note to try and respond with kindness and love the next time, even if you only do it once before losing your mind again, at least you're trying. Baby steps, little by little, start working to be more

11. Patience

loving and patient. You survived combat, you can definitely be a dad, but you have to commit to it.

12. Dinner

Afghanistan 2005

We had gotten to know the Afghan company at the border checkpoint pretty well after a couple months. The company commander was probably working directly for the Taliban as he had sabotaged a couple different ambushes we had set up on the enemy. Their XO was a former mujahedeen fighter who was capable of amazing accuracy with the AK-47 and I brought him along with every single mission. He usually brought along a buddy of his, and the two of them were just as good as any special operations US soldier. They understood fields of fire, CQB, and knew all of our hand and arm signals. There was also a goat herder, a cook, and their logistics guy who we called Smiley because he was always smiling. Seriously, always, even during rocket attacks...always. Smiley invited us to meals almost every day, and I tried to find excuses not to do it every day.

There was one building at the border checkpoint, and that building was the kitchen. It had a hole with a small PVC pipe in it where everything drained out and then flowed downhill to the wadi below. After a few months, it looked like a black sludge river, but when you approached it, the river came alive and billions of flies filled the air in a loud humming sound like an electric car engine. I had no interest in eating anything that came out of that kitchen.

Eventually after a few requests, SSG Walker came and found me to tell me that the Afghans were getting offended by my constant refusals and I really needed to eat with them. So I reluctantly agreed and I told them we could make a day out of it. The morning started with Afghan foot bread and some sort of sweet yogurt paste. It was actually pretty good, and their bread was awesome. After breakfast they had some prayer time and brought a goat to slaughter for the dinner that night.

We walked just outside the wire, in between the gate and the precarious shit hole balance beam and began the ritual killing. The mullah said a prayer as he stood behind the goat with a dull knife in his hand. He then lifted its head and began to slice. The knife was too dull and only made the goat angry without actually killing it. This poor animal was kicking and screaming as they held a rope to keep it from running off. The executioner, now clearly frustrated with his crappy knife, walked over to a rock and, I shit you not, "sharpened" his knife on this rock.

He walked back over to the enraged goat and began slicing and hacking again left to right furiously. He finally broke the goat's skin and started hacking into its throat. When he got to the spine, either his knife was too dull, or it was the custom, but he let the goat lie down on the ground. This animal was still kicking and breathing through the gaping hole in its neck. Blood was going everywhere, and then it puked out of this severed hole. It took a couple minutes for the animal to finally die as it struggled to breathe, and its eyes shifted around furiously. It was hard to watch, and I really just wanted to pull out my sidearm in an act of mercy and put a bullet into its skull. Years later, I made the mistake of watching a beheading video; everything was eerily similar to what I saw that morning in Afghanistan. That goat wasn't done with me though, and it would have its revenge.

We sat down on the floor around a large pan about three feet in diameter piled high with rice and goat meat. I took small bits of bread, which doubled as a utensil and fed myself out of the community bowl. I saw a large cube of meat, about an inch wide and grabbed it zealously. As soon as I took a bite, I realized, I had put a giant chunk of fat in my mouth. My face must have lost color as I locked eyes with SSG Walker sitting in front of me. He could see it based on my expression that I wanted to spit out the bit I had just taken. His eyes widened, he pursed his lips tightly and ever so slightly shook his head. He was right, and I knew it, I couldn't spit this out, not now; I had to eat it. I remember swallowing once and then a second time to swallow my upchuck. My body was already revolting, but I had to fight it.

I don't remember the rest of the meal, nor much else after either. By this point in the deployment we had built ourselves some plywood toilets, so I didn't need to brave the shit pit. The next memory I have is sitting on the toilet, exploding out of my ass and simultaneously projectile vomiting onto the ground in front of the shitter while holding the door open. Every muscle in my core was flexing and it was as though my body wanted get rid of all my internal organs. I was in full on dysentery and I passed out with my pants around my thighs in the fetal position in the dirt and rocks right in front of the makeshift johns. My medic found me there, cleaned me up a bit, and hooked me up to an IV. That was the last meal I had from those guys, and thankfully, they didn't invite me again.

North Carolina 2015

Every night, without fail, there will be something "disgusting" on my son's plate. Every...single...night. It started years ago when he was still a baby. My wife was pressured to start solid foods with him earlier than either of them were ready. I remember her fighting with him over every meal and seeing her in tears trying to get the boy to eat. There was not a trick on the internet or in a book that could help. That boy was going to fight harder than a Gracie in the cage.

The added difficulty to feeding our offspring was that he did not speak until he was almost three years old. He tried to speak, but it was completely unintelligible and he would get even more pissed when we couldn't understand him. We ended up having to put him with a speech pathologist, and that was actually one of the best decisions we made. Once we could understand our little beast, life became much easier.

The most confusing aspect of this is how advanced he is today. Jonathan will sit for hours and build Lego sets for kids twice his age, and he can read absolutely everything. I laughed when he brought home an assignment from Kindergarten about recognizing the alphabet, and he read the instructions to me. Even still, his food choices are infuriating. He likes cheese pizza, but only if he can't see the sauce and he doesn't like the crust either. He likes pasta with butter and parmesan, corn dogs, and fruit. Some days he will eat rice and broccoli, and he loves salmon. He will eat a peanut butter and Jelly sandwich, but only if the edges are cut off. Finally he also…no wait…yeah that's it, that's pretty much all he eats.

We make it a point to sit together at the dinner table every night as a family. We ask each other about our day and it helps the children develop conversational skills. It's an important part of our day, and we try to schedule our activities so that we can all make it to dinner and sit together. By starting the tradition now, as they get older, and life gets crazier, they will know that every night, they are expected to make it to our table for dinner.

Today, however, pretty much every dinner starts the same way: The kids start screaming because play time is over and they need to clean up. Isabella tells me how she "can't" clean up. Baby Ben runs around behind his brother Jonathan pulling out toys that Jonathan has already put away. Jonathan gets frustrated and yells at Ben. I pick up Ben and help them finish cleaning up. We get to the table and Jonathan asks what's for dinner. Immediately after receiving the answer he says, "I don't like that." I say "that's a surprise," and start setting the table. I tell Isabella to take the costume she's wearing off, she throws a fit. She comes back in five minutes in a completely different outfit, but without a shirt. The kids get in their seats and start playing with their placemats like two dimensional light sabers sending crumbs from lunch flying all over the table and the floor. The baby starts screaming. I give him his water bottle and he yells "NO!" I give him his plate and he yells, "NO!" and pushes it away. I hand him a napkin and he yells, "NO!" I hand him his fork and spoon and he yells, "NO!" I walk away and grab another plate. I hear the metal clank of the fork and spoon

12. Dinner

hitting the floor. I walk back with the other kid's plates. Jonathan tells me something on his plate is gross while I pick up Ben's fork and spoon off the ground (he's still screaming). Isabella digs in immediately. Finally my wife and I sit down, make eye contact and start, "how was your day?"

Before I had kids, I thought I could do a better job than most of the parents out there. I was good at everything I set my mind to, why wouldn't I be good at being a parent? Once you become one, then you realize how hard it really is. Let me tell you something right now that every parent should know, but for some reason they don't: NO ONE HAS IT ALL TOGETHER! No one. I don't care how many beautiful pictures they put on Facebook, Instagram, Twitter, or even on their walls at home, none of them have it together. For every one beautiful picture on the wall, there are at least 20 terrible pictures. In fact, when I get a picture from my wife with all three kids smiling at the camera, my first question is always, "how did you get all three to smile at the camera?" I'm seriously in shock when I see that.

So no, you're probably not a failure as a dad. Your friend or neighbor probably doesn't have it any more together than you, and yes, we all struggle with the same thing. How do I nicely tell my kid to stop being a little shit about dinner? The things I've seen kids around the world chomp down because they were starving and you're saying that a steak is "disgusting"! It can send me into a rage, but he's five years old! He doesn't know any better, and even if I explain it, he doesn't care. His entire world is right in front of him, I need to just relax about it. When he gets hungry enough he'll eat.

That's the thing about being a parent, the trick that people need to learn, you sheepdogs in particular. You're used to people immediately listening to you and doing exactly as they are told. You're used to meeting any defiance with escalating force. Now there's a little copy of you running around who isn't afraid of you and willing to defy your every order, and you love them more than you love yourself.

Survival Tip: You will be the type of husband your daughter looks for and the type of husband your son will be.

That's the kicker, you're doing everything in your power to make sure that your kid is better than you are. You want to make sure they have more opportunities than you did, and that

Me and my Daughter Isabella

they are smarter, healthier, and take appropriate risks. You want them to be sooooo different than you…but they're not. There is no magic formula here gents. You're raising a kid who learns from example. They watch your every move and emulate it. They see the pictures on the wall, and they want to do that. If you want your daughter to marry a good man, you better be him. If you want your son to be a great father, you better show him.

Your kids will keep you as their hero, and with everything you've done in life, it will be easy for them to claim you as such. They will take pictures of you to school and show off what a badass their daddy is, and the other kids will agree. So what if you act out at home? What if you're angry and yelling and drunk all the time? What if you let the depression get the best of you and you sit on the couch sulking? What are they going to learn?

Once you have kids, you're not living your life for you anymore, so stop being the center of your own universe. They didn't ask to be here, they deserve the best you have. I get it, you went through some shit, we all did. Get yourself together; make it a point to find help somewhere. If it means sitting on a couch with a psychologist or in a confessional with a priest, whatever works, you need to do it. Stop sitting around feeling sorry for yourself, you're not going to find healing sulking on your couch at the bottom of a bottle.

13. The Schedule

Iraq 2007

When we landed in Iraq and got settled into the FOB, we celebrated my friend's 29th birthday. I remember coming to the realization and giving him so much crap because we were on a 14 month tour. That meant he would celebrate both 29 and 30 in the desert. The last year of his 20's was going to be robbed from him, and I don't think he thought about that before that night. My memory fails me, but we weren't the type to sing happy birthday, so we probably just

handed him a pound cake with a match in it and then gave him shit about it. Those are the best moments in the brotherhood that is the military.

Staff Officer shenanigans in Iraq

The toughest part about a 14 month tour, especially as a staff weenie/fobbit like I was going to be this time around, was figuring out how to spend my time without getting complacent and losing the warrior mentality. I was used to a high-intensity deployment and now I was going to have an actual schedule. Every day will be exactly like the last, and I would probably not encounter the enemy at all. My job now was to plan missions and come up with great ideas to interdict enemy forces, deny them terrain, and do it all with a laptop instead of a rifle; it sucked.

My good friend John Elliott, a former green beret with seven kids who was our PA, taught me how to survive the 14 month sentence: The Schedule. John taught me how to live life overseas by the minute, looking forward only to the next break. It looked generally like this as best I can remember

0500   Wake up/PT

0700   Report to the office

1200   Lunch

1500   Gym

1800   Dinner

2000   Cigar

2200   Sleep

All the "warfighting" happened in between those breaks. Every day, I looked only to the next break in the schedule. It helped me stay focused when I was in the office. Five hours in the morning, one of which was sitting in the Battle Update Brief (BUB), then the afternoon went much faster, a few hours here, a couple there, bada-bing and we're having a cigar in front of our hooch.

For someone who is accustomed to fighting on to the objective, who takes pleasure in the chaos and fog of war, sitting in front of a computer all day while your unit goes and fights the war is torturous. Of course my parents were excited to know that this deployment was going to be a boring monotonous feat of patience, but for me I was simply looking for a way to get outside the wire and find the enemy.

Occasionally we'd have a break in our schedule. I got out of the wire only a handful of times, and we did get into an exchange of fire on one of them. I didn't use the term "firefight" on purpose. You know what I'm talking about, the fifteen second firefight that's about 200 rounds back and forth then everyone waits around trying to figure out what happened and where it came from. I was so stoked at having my chance when the shots started, but just as quickly as they came, it was over and I was heading back to my desk on the FOB.

Occasionally there would be a rare rocket attack, and that was also a nice break in the schedule. Then there was the one time I got a cyst and ended up having to sleep in the hospital for a couple nights, but for the most part, every day from June 2007 until July 2008 was exactly like the one prior.

CONUS Present Day

If you have children, it's imperative you learn the rule of the schedule. This is another aspect of parenting that I learned from my wife. Little kids, much like prisoners and deployed soldiers, need a schedule to rule their life. Having the stability of repeated activity at the same time will do wonders to their expectations and mood throughout the day.

When you do this enough, your kids will help enforce the schedule. They will get tired during nap times, hungry at meal times, and energetic during play times. If you're having trouble getting your kids to sleep, then try out the schedule.

This is a bit of a double edged sword, however, because any straying from the schedule results in pandemonium. We have about an hour of flex, then all hell breaks loose. Kids start screaming and fighting, throwing and kicking, and generally acting like little assholes. I've learned to sympathize with parents when their kid is losing his shit because I know what it's like. You may not remember it, but you were a little asshole to your mom, and your kids will be little assholes to you. It doesn't matter if you think instilling discipline and swatting them every once in a while is going to make a difference, it's not. Your kid will throw a tantrum in public, he will kick and scream and throw himself on the ground as tears pour from his face and no amount of "discipline" on your part will stop the meltdown. It's going to happen, it happens to all of us; the goal is to have it happen more rarely.

Survival Tip: Develop a Schedule

Our kids wake up every day at the same time. They get dressed, eat breakfast and get to watch a short TV show. My wife takes the oldest to school and then she goes to the gym where the other two get to play. After the gym they come home, get more playtime, maybe do some reading, eat lunch and go to bed. After naps they have a snack and go pick up the oldest at school. They come home, watch another show and then get to play some more. I'm usually getting home around this time and I join them for playtime. We then go through the dinner routine that I talked about earlier, watch their final show, and take a bath. After bath we read a book or two and then go to bed. They get about 90 minutes of TV each day, and around six hours of playtime.

If you think I'm full of it and don't want to implement a schedule for the day, at least develop a bedtime routine. This will save your life! Our routine starts at 1900 every day when the kids start their final show which usually runs 30 minutes. As soon as the credits roll, they know they need to take off their clothes to take a bath. I'm in charge of bath time and also getting their jammies on after bath. I get them dressed, and we read a book. Once the book is done, all three kids know it's time to sleep, and usually by 2000 there's silence in our house.

If you want to maintain your sanity, you're going to want to have a regular bedtime and a regular routine for bedtime, otherwise you and your wife will never have time to yourselves. That adds stress to the relationship which is never good. Mommy and Daddy get to hang out for an hour or two after everyone is down where we can have some time just to ourselves. This time to ourselves has been really important to our marriage, and days when we don't get it, I can tell the difference.

Some real talk for a minute...

If you are struggling with things that you have seen, or maybe even done, you cannot afford to have a strained marriage. I know, chicken or the egg, but the best way that I have found is to fix everything around me first, then work on myself. It seems a bit backwards, but you'll never have the time and peace to deal with the demons in your head if you don't have a steady job, or

13. The Schedule

your kids are wearing you out completely, or if you and your wife are always fighting. Tell that angry fucker to sit down, you'll deal with him soon enough, first you need to fix some shit. This advice is only for those of us that are already functioning members of society. Those of us that only we know something is wrong, we jump at loud noises, occasionally we have a bad dream, we get angry easily and struggle with empathy, but for the most part, we can make it day to day.

For some of you, this problem is powerful enough that you need to seek some help; please do. If you're having suicidal thoughts, or can't seem to cope with the weight life has put on you, you need to put this book down and get real help. Twenty-two veterans take their lives every day, don't be a damn statistic because you are too proud to get help. I'm glad you got this book and are actually reading it; now find someone to talk to today. Right now, put this book down and go find some help.

If you have older kids and teenagers, I don't have any help for you yet. Please send me any valuable tips on how to deal with a sassy teenage girl. Particularly for my wife, she already argues with the three year old regularly.

14. Husband

CONUS Present Day

Marriage is the most lasting, personal, and private commitment you will ever make to another human being. This commitment should not be taken lightly, and once it has, you need to really commit to staying with it. I can hear you grumbling already, I understand that this is a team effort, but you need to be a leader of this team. Think of this as an investment in yourself. I have met very few divorced people that would do everything exactly the same way if they had the chance to do it all over again.

Me and my wife Emily

I know how high the divorce rates are for us combat arms guys. I've seen many marriages crumble around me, and although I've never gone through it myself, I've been a keen study of the failures of my peers. I have counseled many soldiers and seen enough of these fail to be able to identify the warning signs early on.

The goal of this chapter is not to chastise you in any way. If you are already divorced, I want you to realize that you are not alone and maybe see the problems to avoid the next time. If you are currently struggling, then I hope that I can offer some words of wisdom that have been given to me to help you get your marriage on the right path. If things are going well in your marriage, then maybe you can learn some additional tips to further strengthen your relationship. Finally if you have never been married, maybe this will help you get into the right mindset from the beginning to avoid the pitfalls that so many of us have fallen into.

Survival tip: Treat your marriage with respect

Too many couples are treating their marriage like a transaction or a contract instead of a commitment. They are approaching the relationship selfishly, only when the other person is providing something will they act in kind. I've seen it on both sides, men and women cheating on each other regularly, always seeking the next exciting event. The irony of it all is that they blame the other person for not treating them well enough, or not doing enough, or not being enough, when the whole time they were just looking for an excuse to let their eyes wander. If you don't treat your marriage with respect, no one else will and that includes your partner.

We live in a society that is saturated with lust and sex at every turn, if you don't make it a point to look at your wife, your eyes will find something to look at. It always starts small, a conversation, maybe a lunch date, and then you begin to compare and finally you act because your partner wasn't satisfying you. Let me ask you something jackass, what the fuck were you doing for your partner during this time? Were you busy playing video games, drinking with the boys, working on a car, or golfing? Men treat their marriage like shit and wonder why it goes to shit.

This is the purest act of selfishness I see over and over again. Ask a cheater why they cheated, "well she..." No dumbass, "she" nothing, your marriage was your responsibility and you failed. If you think marriage is going to be easy because you're in love, then you're delusional. It takes work, but like all good things in life, it's worth the reward. The harder it is to get something, the more valuable it is. Marriage is a prize, your wife is a prize, and you won her, now you have to keep her.

I fall short in this almost daily. I have a hard time thinking about someone other than myself, and the more that I focus on me, the worse it is for *us*. I know some of you out there are not religious, but let me tell you that this is another area where God has really helped me. When I focus on God, I am reminded that this is not about me, and I realize that when I take a servant's heart, not only am I rewarded in life, but I'm also rewarded in my marriage.

My parents divorced when I was 19 years old. They stayed together for me, and then my father faltered. He started thinking about himself and forgot about his family. It was tough for our relationship for a long time after what he did to my mother. It took me years to forgive him and begin the process of repairing our relationship. I was angry for a very long time, and anger is an emotion that comes exceptionally easily to me. Selfishly I don't want my kids to feel towards me what I felt towards my own father. It would kill me if my boy went off to war and was getting in firefights but refused to talk to me at all and treated me as though I didn't even exist.

You need to learn to control your thoughts and set your mind on your partner instead of everyone else. It's not going to be better with someone else, you know why? Because you are the problem. Yeah, I said it. If you do the same thing with this new lady soon you'll get bored again and start looking somewhere else. It's the same reason why Hugh Hefner can't even be satisfied with triplets, the dude is only looking to satisfy himself. He is acting in utmost selfishness, and that gentlemen, is not rewarding.

Survival Tip: Fight fair

You and your wife are a team. You can't win an argument by being a dick, because then the team loses. My mother used to tell me, "keep your words soft and sweet because you never know when you're going to have to eat them." I still fail at this because I'm a smartass and incredibly self-centered. I know what will cut the deepest, and I don't like to lose, so I will pull out the knives during an argument with the sole purpose of hurting her. I am very good at sending her in tears out of the room, but that is not satisfying at all. I feel no better, no more satisfied, and my relationship is not stronger at all. I've done nothing beneficial for anyone and I've only caused hurt and pain to our relationship. To what end? Why did I do that?

I've begun to ask myself a question when I feel the fury rising inside: "What would I do if someone other than me made my wife feel this way?" Let that one linger for a second. If your wife came home crying because some stranger in the parking lot did the exact same thing you just did, how would you react? Would you be letting the beast out of his cage for one more round? I know I would. So stop it, stop arguing to win, and start fighting fair.

Make sure you understand what she's upset about before you start spouting off at the mouth. Repeat back what she's saying and make sure she agrees that you understand why she's angry. She is your queen, treat her as such. You want respect, and often you demand it, make sure you are giving it to your partner as well. Often times we are very good at keeping our cool and being cordial with complete strangers, but when it comes to the ones we love, our patience is short and so are our words.

If you're not good at this, like me, then you better be good at saying you're sorry. This I have down pat; I'm excellent at apologizing. I'm short to think, short to listen, and quick to speak, which is a losing combination. I'm also quick to realize that I screwed up and apologize. Some days I think this is the only reason she's decided to stay with me over the years. Apologizing isn't easy either, but because I keep reminding myself that it's about the team and not about me, it comes faster.

As an intelligence officer, it was important for me to be able to think like the enemy. I had to learn as much as I could about a stranger, and then place myself in his shoes to figure out what he would probably do. That skill and training has been useful in marriage, not because my wife is the enemy, but because I have had to learn to think like someone else. One way or another, most of you have done the same thing. Even something as simple as digging a foxhole required you to examine your defenses from the point of view of another person. I try, whenever she's upset, to think about the argument through her eyes. Doing that is a valuable tool in realizing what a jackass I'm being, and it makes it easier to apologize. Being angry and violent is easy, it takes more courage to withstand those urges and pursue peace.

Survival Tip: Have fun

I've seen couples, and even sometimes mine, become roommates instead of partners. Have some fun with each other. Pick something she likes and do it with/for her, and have a good attitude about it. My wife loves TV shows and we have been known to blow through a Netflix series in a couple weeks. One of the shows that I watch for her is Mindy. I fought this for a while, because I'm a man damn it and I'm too good to sit around and watch silly chick flick TV shows, but it was important to her. Frankly, if you jackoffs think I'm less of a man because I spend time with my wife watching a show she loves, I really couldn't care less. I'm not living my life for you douchebags. How many of you care more about what your buddies think than what your partner thinks? You're an idiot if you do.

A couple days ago I took the kids outside to get some energy out and a game of freeze tag developed. Now the rules of freeze tag when you play with three people under five are fluid at best. Basically I'm "it" and my kids run around while I chase them. Momma was inside making dinner, and I was hoping to give her a reprieve from the minions for a bit, when she came out of the front door and started running around with us. For fifteen minutes we laughed as we ran around the house surprising each other at corners and watching the baby try and run across the grass. That is the stuff that matters gents. Moments like that are what make life worth living. Ensure that you make time for fun.

Those are the moments that my kids will remember and they are the moments that my wife looks most beautiful to me. She wasn't wearing a fancy dress, she didn't have high-heels on, her makeup wasn't particularly done for the day, but my heart skipped a beat when I looked at her. Seeing her big smile as she picked up the baby, the two of them laughing as the sun lit up her blue eyes and danced across her dirty blonde hair... yeah, I married up for sure. Plus her ass looked great in those yoga pants.

Gentlemen, it's important to keep the right mindset in your marriage:

- Remember that you are part of a team
- Remember that marriage is a commitment and not a contract
- Think about how she feels
- Are you treating her how you expect others to treat her?
- Respect your marriage
- Have fun

Your marriage can be the greatest cause of joy or consternation in your life, it's up to you.

15. Empathy

Afghanistan 2005

I stood in the TOC listening intently to the radio. My company was in a major firefight and I was hours away pulling QRF for FOB Salerno. With every transmission, my heart sunk more, I could hear the explosions in the background and CPT Teague's voice was strained and agitated; Teague never got that way. This was probably one of the largest fights we had ever been in, and I was stuck listening to it play out, plotting positions on the map, trying to get an idea of the fight. I asked to take my QRF out there several times, but Teague had not requested it, and the battlefield was already chaotic enough before adding us into the mix, so there I stood, listening to my brothers get shot up.

The 9-line medevac request came through, and I copied it alongside the battle captain. I remember the confirmation that the bird had taken off. SFC Anderson looked at me, "I'm going to meet it at the aid station." I nodded and he left. The battle continued to rage, and my request to join the fight was denied again. When we heard the medevac had landed in Salerno, I waited a few more minutes to make sure they weren't going to let us go help, then I left the TOC to head to the aid station.

It was a long straight road, about a quarter mile with tents to my left and the LZ's on my right. As I made the walk, SGT Fredsti drove up in a gator and stopped right in front of me. I could see the look on his face and I knew it was bad. I didn't even have time to ask a question before he spoke, "It's sergeant Nixon sir. He's dead." I couldn't even respond. I looked at him and nodded, and he drove off.

I stood there on the road for a while, not taking a step anywhere, just looking into the desert thinking about Travis Nixon. I would never hear his laugh again. I would never get to talk or joke or smoke with him again. I thought about his wife and the news she was about to receive. I thought about the boys still fighting that didn't know yet. I thought about the other men we had lost. I remembered standing in the TOC listening to Pete Vanjgel call in a 9-line for Jim Oschner as they gave him CPR; I knew he wouldn't make it. I thought about Gunny Theodore Clark who was killed by an IED and getting the news while sitting on the edge of my cot watching a movie. I remembered Victor Cervantes who was killed rescuing my guys just days before going back home. I just stood there in silence.

I finally took a breath and kept walking towards the aid station. It was the longest quarter mile I had ever walked. When I walked in, I could see the floor was covered in blood. There was a nurse with a mop trying to wipe it up, but she was crying almost uncontrollably and making very little progress. SFC Anderson was just to my right filling out the paperwork. I had never seen sadness on that man's face before this day. He looked at me and his eyes were bright red, neither of us said anything. I think I was still in shock.

A few hours later, one of the nurses offered to let us say one final goodbye. Several of us were escorted into a back room. She unzipped the body bag and there was Travis' body. I could see the hole of the fatal wound just next to his shoulder; he was in the prone position when he got hit. She only unzipped it halfway, but we knew the round exited near his hip. According to some of the stories I've heard, as he was being carried out, he told the guy carrying him, Patrick Trattles, that he wasn't going to make it. I've heard similar stories of soldiers knowing that death had arrived to take them, and I've wondered how they know.

Travis was the first friend whom I saw lifeless. I said a prayer over his body, but it was clear Travis wasn't there. He had moved on, his body looked like a vessel, it reminded me of Travis, but there was no doubt he had moved on. I felt a sense of peace, and I felt really close to God that day. It was the day I realized that I was mortal, and one day, I'd be lying on a table just like Travis, the remnants of a broken vessel that could no longer contain my soul. I knew God would be there to receive me, and the my memory in those left behind would be all that remains of the efforts I put forth in this life.

This realization has a way of making so many things seem trivial, but it reprioritized what I valued in life. When I was just a boy, my father taught me the importance of being a man of principle. He told me that men can take away your possessions, your loved ones, even your life, but the only thing that they can't take away, the only thing that only you can give away is your principles. It didn't sink in immediately, for years even, but as I walked from the aid station with my friends in silence back to our hooches, I began to ponder what the hell I was living my life for. I thought about Travis and wondered what people would think of me when I'm gone. Travis was a better man than me; many men are better than me. For some reason God let me continue and he has blessed me far beyond what I deserve. I fall short every day.

Travis is not the only friend I have lost. If you read the acknowledgements, then you will see there are many others, too many others. Through the years I have gotten the phone calls: Kislow killed himself, Loeza didn't make it, Preciado had an accident, Beezley chose to end it, Joe Schultz won't come home.

As recently as last year my close friend Mike Donahue, a dedicated husband and father of three was killed. I was in a hotel on a business trip when I got the phone call from Jim Schreiner, our old S3. The conversation didn't last very long,

neither of us really had much to say. After sitting in the room by myself for a few minutes in silence, I walked to the hotel bar and had a couple drinks,

Me and Mike Donahue in Iraq

bummed a cigarette off of someone there and sat outside staring at the stars. I didn't cry... I couldn't. I guess I've already cried all the tears I can. I thought about his family and my heart broke for those kids... I have three kids also... those poor kids. I finished my drink and went back to my room. I laid in the dark, smelling of whisky and Marlboro, staring at the ceiling for hours until my alarm went off. I took a shower, put on my John Deere uniform, drove to the farm show, and strained to smile all day.

This is the pain we carry that most people out there don't understand. So few have sustained the magnitude and recurrence of loss that we have. We don't want to talk about it, but we certainly think about it often. At least once a week, something happens that makes me think about a lost friend, or a gold star family... think about them, miss them, wonder why I was spared, move on with my day... I was given the gift of life, I better live it.

It's hard to feel empathy when you don't even feel anymore. Empathy is the emotion I struggle with the most, I can laugh, I can fee love, I can very easily feel anger, frustration, happiness, etc. But Empathy does not come easily. I can tell when I get news from someone that they want me to feel empathy. For them I put on a show, I know what I should say, how I should act, even what I should feel, but I don't feel it. I'm sorry your pet died... what's for dinner? His grandfather had a stroke? How old was he? Wow, the old man made it far. We're all going to die, as far as I'm concerned, making it to 90 is winning. My wife hates it when I talk about death; she says I'm too comfortable with the prospect.

I want a keg and a party at my funeral. I already had an awesome life; I want people to celebrate that. I got to live on several continents and I've seen the world and its wonders. I've made friends who are closer to me than family. I married a

143

beautiful woman and had three amazing kids. Don't mourn my death, I lived hard, and if death comes and finds me tomorrow, he knows I'm not afraid. We've already stood face to face before, the next time I'm going to smile at his ugly mug. I don't yearn for death, though. I hope for the sake of my babies that I've got many years ahead of me; as long as my mind and body are strong, I wouldn't mind sticking around to see how things turn out.

Look, I don't really have any good survival tips for you here, I just want you to know that you're not alone. I know how you feel, and I've felt it too. One thing I do keep telling myself is that I owe it to the guys that didn't come home to actually live my life. I better enjoy every God damn minute I get on this planet and make the best of it, because I know 17 other guys who didn't get that chance and their families would give anything to have one more shitty day with them, and they would love every minute of it.

Life is good gents, and it's worth living. I have my reason to go on, what's yours?

16. Buddy Set! I got you covered!

Iowa 2012

Remember "fuckhead" from earlier in the book? He was the guy who called me a liar in a discipline hearing because he was a coward and didn't want to face the consequences of his actions, and I got investigated because of it. Anyway, if you don't remember, you can go back to Chapter 4.

There is another part of that story that I saved for this section. I was furious that day. It was a special kind of anger that I have only felt a handful of times in my life. It is a feeling that fills my entire body, coursing through my veins, adrenaline surges through my body, and my hands begin to shake. My breathing gets shallow, my eyes narrow, I'm ready to attack, poised for violence. The smallest thing can result in the biggest reaction when that's happening to me. I was wearing my rage on my face, and few people even engaged me as I waited.

Luckily I had a really good supervisor who saw that I was enraged that day. Mike Tucker walked through the HR department when I was waiting on the investigation. He was walking by and did a double-take and stopped. I shook my head and without a word, he knew it was not the time and place. He moved on knowing he was going to ask me what happened later.

Mike pulled me into his office later, closed the door and let me say everything I wanted to. I'm not sure that I've ever cursed as much as I did in those 20 minutes, but I didn't hold back at all. He was incredibly reasonable and explained to me why I needed to calm down and get it together in a way that made sense. He knew me well enough to know what mattered to me and in no uncertain terms, made it clear that losing control could cost me my job, and it wasn't fair to my family if I did that.

If you can find a guy like Mike Tucker in your job, I highly recommend it. Mike was not a veteran, but he is an awesome guy who actually cares about his employees and their well-being. He's also really good at translating civilian values into military ones, and at a time in my life when I was inexperienced with that, Mike quite literally saved my career. Today, even though I'm thousands of miles away, I still have monthly phone calls with Mike and he is my formal mentor. It's great to know that there's someone I can fully trust to be uncensored with and there won't be repercussions.

Survival Tip: Don't go it alone

Gents, this may be the most important piece of advice I can give you, and it probably shouldn't be buried this far in the book, but it's my story, so I'll tell it like I want. Stop and think for one second, can you think of a single job in the military where you don't have a buddy or someone to support you? One guy can pull security for a day or two, two guys can go forever at 50%. You need someone there to cover you while you move, and your strength increases exponentially for each unit. Think about the destructive power of a division versus a squad. You might be the next Audie Murphy, but there will be days where you're going to need somebody and it's not your wife. She's the one person you have dedicated your life to in the most permanent and personal decision you will ever make, I get that, but she's not your battle buddy. If you start talking about your failures with your wife, she's going to try and nurture you, and that's not what you need.

You need to find at least one other guy that thinks like you, and it's even better if that guy is not a veteran. Having a veteran battle buddy is important too, and most of us have those already. I know for a fact that as you read that sentence, at least one guy came to mind that you can call right now, no matter what time it is, and if you're struggling, he's going to talk to you. That guy is important, but just as important is to have someone that doesn't come from the same world as us, but shares some of the same values. Those guys can serve as a sounding board and also as a "terp". They are able to hear what you are saying, understand it, then tell you what the rest of the world is seeing in this situation. I am very blessed to have several of these relationships.

I've probably dropped too many F-Bombs to have credibility in this regard, especially with my fleeting references to God, but I am a practicing Christian. I haven't always been, and I am far cry from where I should be, but my faith has not only helped me to cope with and defeat my demons, but it has also introduced me to the men that would become my battle buddies.

One of these guys is the assistant pastor at a large church in Ottumwa. Cy McMahon is a big guy, somewhere over six foot and probably around 220 pounds. He is loud, funny, and will give you a welcoming hug and giant slap on the back as you enter the church. When he's in the building you will know about it. Cy was a salesman for Pella windows, making six figures, traveling all over the country when he got the call to become a pastor. He took a 70% pay cut and moved to Ottumwa, Iowa with his family. I've done some bold things, but I respect a man that can do that. Ask him today about it and he will tell you it's the best move he ever made.

Semi-annually the church in Iowa put out a list of small groups for people to join. The pastor goes through a speech about how small groups are transformative and strongly recommends them. Because I'm as stubborn as a mule, it was a long time before I finally decided to take the speech seriously. I decided to join a men's group that met at 0545 in a local coffee shop. It was there that I learned that Cy was more than just a funny guy. He wrestled with many of the same hardships I did, and as he opened up about them, I realized that talking about these things didn't make him weak at all but he came at them from a position of strength.

As killers we are trained to ignore pain. I dislocated my knee three times in an hour in SF selection because I kept putting my kneecap back in place and I didn't want to quit. I told you about Ted Smith who was shot in the face and kept fighting, and most of us have seen the pictures of amputees going back overseas or doing Spartan races. Pain is not something we shy away from or fear, and sometimes we welcome it; it's how we know our limbs are still there. The problem is that we end up ignoring emotional pain as well.

Being open about feelings is not something we killers are good at. We may break down and cry during roll call and taps, but then you wipe the few tears off your face and you move on. I know in combat, showing that kind of strength is important, but at some point you need to heal, and you can't do that if you don't address the wound.

For months I went to that group and listened to other people open up, and I shared intellectual insights about the topics, but I never got personal. One day, I can't remember what the topic of conversation was, but I was transported back to the mountains in Afghanistan. After a firefight that resulted in multiple injuries and one death, we set up an ambush over the fallen enemy. Eventually the corpses rotted out and no one came to retrieve them. A couple months later, in August, we returned to the scene. I hadn't been a part of that fight that particular day where two of my soldiers were shot. I sat next to a radio and listened to it for hours; it was the worst day of my entire military career without a doubt. When we went back, my guys were walking me through the battle, step by step, on the terrain.

Finally we turned a corner and were hit by the smell of death. I looked down and saw the skeleton of a man that had been ripped apart by coyotes. His clothes were torn and there were clear bite marks on his limbs. The animals and the Afghan sun had wiped his flesh almost entirely off his body. In the center of his skull, right between the eyes was the distinguishable kill shot. One of my soldiers reached down and picked up his skull. As he lifted it up, the spine and jaw followed. Only one side of the jaw was held on and it swung to the side. The spine was also somehow still attached as well and dangled freely. We all laughed hysterically and made jokes about how my soldier looked like scorpion from Mortal Combat holding the skull. He stuck out his tongue and a few of us took pictures with the skull.

That was only one of a few bodies I saw that year, and not the only one that I stood over and laughed about, but for some reason, he was the one I thought about in a coffee shop before the sun rose in a small town in Iowa. I finally came face to face with the monster inside me, my Mr. Hyde reared his ugly head. I've killed men and rejoiced in their death, but worse than that, I've defiled their corpses for fun. That was someone's son, maybe he was a father, or a husband. Someone loved him, and he fought for his side bravely. That day, like most days, we were better, and for that he lost his life.

I didn't share the whole story with the group, all I could get out was, "I've stood over dead men and laughed," before a knot formed in my throat and tears welled up in my eyes. Since that day I've gotten better about sharing some of the things I've done, heck I'm writing a whole book about it. I'm still not good at exploring feelings, but I've realized that it's not just the sick shit we saw that we bring home, sometimes it's the sick shit we did that scares us more.

I want you to find a battle buddy that you can share some of your stories with. You're not going to find healing at the bottom of a whisky bottle, that numbness is only temporary. Find that guy you trust and begin to open up, it's amazing what happens when you shed light on the dark corners of your life. I've been able to forgive myself, but I've also become aware of what I'm capable of doing. By opening up about my beast, I've been able to put

16. Buddy Set! I got you covered!

him in the cage, and unless you can control him, he will overtake you.

Final Thoughts

I hope that you have found some utility in this book. If you liked this book and thought it was useful, take a couple minutes and send me a message. I want to hear about your story. Tell me about what you liked, what you didn't like, what rang true for you, and even where you think I'm full of shit. I wrote this for you, so tell me what you thought, head to www.conusbattledrills.com or on twitter @conusbattle or even CONUS Battle Drills on Facebook.

If you are thinking about getting out, you should be making a plan, figuring out where you want to live, how much you want to make, where you want to work, and you have reached out to head hunters. Those of you thinking of going to college are re-evaluating your degree and making sure that it's the right path for you. The rest of us are figuring out new and creative ways to make our degrees relevant. If you're already out, maybe you've found some new ways to navigate the pitfalls so many veterans fall into at work.

I hope that you have taken some of the lessons in part two and begun to apply them as well. Learning to cage the beast is a daunting task sometimes, but our children and wives deserve our best. Play with your babies and laugh with them. Make time with your wife, and make a commitment to your marriage. Finally, find that battle buddy that can be a sounding board for you, shed light on those demons.

Final Thoughts

Most of all, I want you to know that you are not alone in this battle. In some form or fashion, every one of us has some struggles that we go through. I want you to know there is an entire community of great men out there to support you. Call on any one of them, and you'll see what I mean. Also, be that person for someone else. Twenty-two vets commit suicide every day, we need to make a concerted effort to look out for each other; no one else is going to do it.

There are certain days of the year that I wake up in a bad mood. June 10th, September 16th, October 29th, then there's 9/11, Veterans day or Memorial day, sometimes it happens on Independence day, and even Thanksgiving. Most of you can understand already what those days mean to me, and you probably have similar days on your calendar where you take a few extra minutes to think of your friends who didn't take that beautiful flight home with you. It's on these days that I get up extra early to spend some time by myself. Having that time to pray and reflect, helps me prepare for the world that doesn't understand me, but it also helps me be more thankful for the things that I do have.

I have plenty of food in my belly (evidenced by the fact that I quickly became a fat slob after I got out), a roof over my head, hot showers, a hot wife, three beautiful genius kids, a regular job, and some really cool stories. One day I will tell my children about the great men that their father knew and fought with. I will tell them stories of heroism, bravery, selflessness, and loss. They will know what Arlington is really about when we stand over several graves and tell stories of champions whose blood was shed in service to our great country. They will understand why I get goose bumps every time I hear the national anthem and one day they will get them too.

God Bless you Gentlemen!

Acknowledgements

Mike Donahue's Memorial in Afghanistan

I want to start by thanking the US Military for being such a big part of my life. The US Army gave my father a way to pay for his doctorate degree and support our family at the same time on account of him being a Sergeant in the 82nd. When he later joined the US Navy, they sent us around the world and I learned several languages and got to see sights that most people will only ever see in books. The US Army gave me a chance to leave college without any debt, taught me so much about myself, and helped me become the man I am today.

I want to thank the men and women of the 82nd Airborne. The 82nd is a culture in and of itself, and one that if you haven't been there it's particularly hard to understand. We're all in the Army, but there's something special about being in America's Guard of Honor. A large portion of our Special Operations forces come from soldiers who were once paratroopers in the 82nd, running up and down Ardennes and jumping into Sicily DZ. You are a fierce bunch, and I'm proud to have been in your ranks.

I want to extend a special thank you to the Devil Brigade past and present. I also want to thank the German Officer in Anzio in WWII who gave the 504th got its iconic name calling them "devils in baggy pants." I still carry a sense of pride when I talk about the history of bravery of the Devils. I still hop up in excitement when watching "A Bridge Too Far", Robert Redford's prayer as the 504th crosses the river in broad daylight brings a smile to my face; we haven't changed much since. Particularly I want to thank the White Devils who are always ready to answer their nation's call. Being a White Devil carried a certain expectation of excellence that catapulted me to be my best self because I was surrounded by the best men.

I want to thank my fellow Lieutenants, Will Brown, Don Bangler, Patrick Clancy, Kareem Fernandez, Mike Filanowski, Brendan Fitzgerald, Micah Neibauer, and Peter Vangjel. You guys were a strong support network, and as we all inevitably did, comparing myself to you always pushed me harder. I had examples of great leadership, fitness, and bravery, in everything you guys did. You taught me more than I can give you credit for and will all be cherished friends.

I would like to thank the men of Bravo Company. You are the toughest group of sons of bitches I ever had the pleasure of serving with. The things I saw you accomplish in a short year in Afghanistan, still baffle me to this day. I can read stories of bravery and understand what the authors are describing in great detail because I saw you do it. Of the 120 men that made up our great company, you showed your mettle earning several Silver

Acknowledgements

Stars, Bronze Stars with Valor, ARCOMs with Valor and Purple Hearts. I salute every single one of you!

To the men of 3rd platoon, although I was totally undeserving of the honor, I'm thankful to have had the opportunity to be your leader. You men made my job easy, and even when I was in it I knew, I had already hit the pinnacle of my military career within the first week of arriving in the 82nd. I want to thank each of you Aguilar, Allbaugh, Bolobanic, Brooks, Butler, Chiruck, Coca, Collazo, Emch, Harrel, Hobbs, Kirkland, Klaysmat, Lambert, Lewis, Loughry, McHugh, Mignone, Moore, Morton, O'Connell, Sang, Schroll, Smith (both of you), Stinson, and Zimmerman. My four squad leaders, Jeff Carrol, Johnny Walker, Adam Flynn, and Steve Bruzinski, watching you lead your squads was a true pleasure, and getting to go on missions with you was always an honor.

For Steve Anderson I have a special thank you. You kept me out of trouble and called me out on my bullshit. I watched you carefully and learned something every day. There are many that survived Afghanistan only because of your leadership and fearlessness. Our platoon was lucky to have your grumpy ass, and I'm thankful for it.

Brandon Teague, the company commander who became a legend, a legend who inspired a movement. The men would joke: WWTD, but us LT's actually thought it. From the moment we met when you checked my left shoulder then offered me a beer, until even today, your opinion still matters greatly to me. You accepted no less than a 300 APFT score and loved to torture us with Coolyconch runs. You sent us deep into the heart of the enemy and taught us to control the battlefield. I felt no fear in executing an order from you. There is no doubt or shake in my voice to say I would follow you into the pits of hell; I already have.

James Schreiner, you were the S3 that taught me the valuable skills that pay my bills today! I will never forget your words, "you have access to the calendar Louis, figure out what to do next on your own. You don't need to ask me." You taught me how to plan, how to write, how to build presentations, and how to account for all the circumstances. You taught me patience, and how to navigate sensitive social situations with people that weren't infantrymen. You showed me how to mitigate my f-bombs and that there is still value and honor as a staff weenie…albeit not quite as much. Nearly every day as a program manager, I go back to that year in Iraq and think of the lessons I learned from you.

Clif Prat or Leonidas as we called you, you told me one day, "Marry her. What are you afraid of?" It was so simple yet so impacting. I spent months going over your words before I realized I was falling in love with Emily and I was using the fear of the future as a crutch. You broke down the barriers in my own mind which allowed for the stupendous blessings of my family pour upon me. I would have missed out on so much if it weren't for you. Thank you.

To the Raiders, Yancey and Everage, Jon Gutauskas, John Gillette, David Virginia, and Josh Brown, training with you guys helped me get through Ranger school and prepared me to lead men in combat. Also Geoff Fahringer, the firefighter, helicopter pilot, sheriff, pastor, who showed me to stop making excuses and just go after my dreams.

Acknowledgements

John Elliott, the guy who created the beast and helped me build the schedule to survive our Iraq deployment. Although I didn't make it through selection, you taught me what I'm capable of achieving with some hard work and effort. You were a great friend and mentor, and I still look to you as an example of a father.

Steve Bartkowski and Matt Gilbert, the Trifecta, the tribunal. I wouldn't be married and have these beautiful babies if it wasn't for you two jokers. I had a great time every day with you, and I still consider you my brothers.

Mike Tucker, I actually owe you my job. Were it not for your level head when I was losing it, I would have either gotten myself fired or quit John Deere. I am so very lucky to have had you as a supervisor when I was a hot-headed veteran entering a union shop. You listened to me earnestly, and you challenged me fearlessly, which was definitely what I needed. I am so very thankful for your mentorship and friendship as well.

Cy McMahon, the funny preacher man who could see right through me. You knew exactly how to push me to open up, and you always led by example. When I think of a Godly man and what he should be, I will always think of you. It takes courage to face an enemy on the battlefield, but it also takes courage to leave everything behind to pursue that which you know is right. I began the process of internal healing thanks to you, and without that, this book would never have happened.

To the men who we lost, SFC Cervantes, SFC Oschner, SSG Nixon, GySGT Clark, SFC Stoddard, SSG Fredsti, CPT Schultz, SGT Dayton, SSG Loeza, SFC Preciado, SPC Katzenberger, 2LT Andrews, and most recently MAJ Donahue, I hope that I

159

can live a life worthy of your sacrifice. I pray for your families, that they may find some peace in your absence. I think of you every single day, and that is not an exaggeration. Although I only wear one name on my wrist, he symbolizes every one of you. I miss you all, the world is missing a few good men. I promise to take my children to Arlington one day and introduce them to the heroes that their daddy had the distinct pleasure of knowing. Until we meet again gentlemen.

To those who lost their battle with the demons in their minds, Kislow, Beezely, Evans, and Lawrence, I wrote this thinking about you. I thought about the battles you were fighting, how you felt alone and helpless. I thought about the twenty-two other veterans that make the same choice every day, and it motivated me to do something to help; this book is my contribution. If there are any of you thinking of making the same choice, please reach out to a buddy. Life is precious, YOUR life is precious, and there are many out there that care for you. We were battle buddies before, we still are, call us anytime.

To my brother Chad Shields, without whom I wouldn't have even graduated college. You were my rock when I had no one else, and we became family by choice, a bond so much stronger than blood. Even though you knew every one of my secrets, familiar with the depths of my own depravity, you still chose to grace me with your friendship. Sitting one afternoon for hours in a TGI Fridays convincing me not to quit college, laughing with me all through Ranger School and our deployment in Afghanistan, to being roommates for a time in Bragg, are all key moments in defining who I am today. I was always in second place behind you, but I didn't mind being behind such a worthy man.

Acknowledgements

To my parents and grandparents, I thank you for all the sacrifices you made to get us to the USA. I thank you for being great examples to me and my children. I have many reasons to be proud of my heritage thanks to what you have done. I cherish the lessons learned over the years.

Jonathan, Isabella, and Benjamin, my beautiful babies, one day I'll share everything with you. I will talk to you about great men and impress upon you the importance of living a life of principle. We are all hear because your dad was spared a great sacrifice, we owe it to those amazing men to leave a legacy worth dying for.

Emily, my love, thank you for your patience as I worked on this project. I'm not deserving of a woman like you, but I'm thankful God put you in my path. I'm thankful that our little Jonathan used his "super power" and made us a family. I hope to have many more years of driving you insane.

Your Workbook

Survival Tips

1. Find a headhunter
2. Read Job postings
3. Get plenty of rest and stay focused for the next 48 hours, your future depends on it!
4. Find purpose in your work
5. During a recession, pick a recession proof company
6. All your interview answers should be in the STAR format- Situation Task Action Result
7. Learn everyone's job
8. In order to move up, you need to move sideways
9. Who you know is just as important as what you know.
10. Chill out, bullets aren't flying, people aren't dying. Take it in stride bro.
11. Silence is your friend, especially when you're angry
12. Don't yell
13. If you want to encourage cultural change, take it in baby steps
14. Make time every single day to spend with your kids.
15. Your family is not a threat, don't treat them like one.
16. You will be the type of husband your daughter looks for and the type of husband your son will be.
17. Develop a Schedule
18. Treat your marriage with respect
19. Fight fair
20. Have fun
21. Don't go it alone

The Four Big Questions

1. Are your finances in order?

Here is my budget template zeroed out. If you think it's useful go ahead and use it, or make your own that is more relevant for you.

Income	Expense		Section Totals
	Monthly Budget		
Income	Expense		Section Totals
Pay		$	
	Mortgage/Tax/Insurance/Escrow	$	$
	Utilities:	$	$
	Electric	$	
	Telephone	$	
	TV/Internet	$	
	Water	$	
	Yard	$	
	Pest Control	$	
	Personal:	$	$
	Groceries	$	
	Clothing Kids	$	
	Clothing Me	$	
	Furniture	$	
	Storage	$	
	Personal Care	$	
	Transportation:	$	$
	Tax & Registration	$	
	Gasoline	$	
	Insurance	$	
	Maintenance	$	
	Recreation:	$	$
	Gym	$	
	Workout Clothes/Shakes/Equipment	$	
	Dining Out	$	
	Movies/Concerts/Events	$	
	Babysitter	$	
	Charitable Donations:	$	$
	Church	$	
	Cash	$	$
	Savings	$	
	Total	$	

2. Do you know why you're getting out?

_____
_____
_____
_____
_____
_____

3. Do you know where you want to live?

Remember the tradeoff!

_____
_____
_____
_____
_____
_____

4. Do you know what you want to do?

_____
_____
_____
_____
_____
_____

My Interview Stories

Tell me about a time…

1.
S_____
_____
_____

T_____
_____
_____

A_____
_____
_____
_____
_____

R_____
_____
_____
_____

2.
S_____
_____
_____

My Interview Stories

T_____
_____
_____

A_____
_____
_____
_____
_____
_____

R_____
_____
_____

3.
S_____
_____
_____

T_____
_____
_____

A_____
_____
_____
_____
_____

R_____
_____

_____
_____

4.
S_____
_____
_____

T_____
_____
_____

A_____
_____
_____
_____
_____

R_____
_____
_____
_____

Resources

These are just a few of the locations that I have found to be really useful and many of the lessons throughout the book were either learned or inspired from here. This is clearly not a fully comprehensive list, but it's a place for you to get started in your search.

FOR IMMEDIATE HELP:

Suicide Hotline 1-800-273-8255

Employment
- Veterans Resource Locator- https://www.veteranscrisisline.net
- Hire Our Heroes- https://hireourheroes.org/veterans/resources/
- Lucas Group- http://www.lucasgroup.com/
- Orion International- http://www.orioninternational.com/military-job-seekers/
- Bradley-Morris-http://www.bradley-morris.com/bmi_candidates.html

Financial
- Dave Ramsey- http://www.daveramsey.com/fpu/
- Free Budget Planner- http://www.moneyhelp.org.au/tools-tips/budget-planner/

- USAA® Money Manager-
  https://www.usaa.com/inet/pages/money_manager_informati
  onal_landing?akredirect=true

Relationships

- iMarriage-http://www.amazon.com/IMarriage-Andy-
  Stanley/dp/1590527305
- Focus on the Family-
  http://www.focusonthefamily.com/marriage
- All Pro Dad- http://www.allprodad.com/
- Dr. James Dobson-
  http://www.drjamesdobson.org/blogs/the-fatherhood-
  challenge
- Manna Church (based near Ft. Bragg)-
  https://www.everymanministries.com/playlist/pastor-manna-
  church-michael-fletcher-michael-fletcher

Index

Lucas Group, 21, 22, 24, 25, 29, 33

M

manager, 10, 19, 24, 26, 30, 38, 39, 70, 72, 73, 76, 134
marriage
marriages, 5, 113
MOS, 19, 39

P

pitfalls, 3, 4, 6, 113, 130

R

rage, 44, 53, 54, 97, 106, 119, 124
Ranger, 5, 12, 13, 28, 34, 35, 42, 69, 92, 94, 135, 137
resume, 3, 21, 22, 23, 24, 25, 80, 81

S

safety, 13, 36, 43, 52, 53
salary, 4, 16, 22, 29, 81, 82
STAR, 22, 31, 32

stereotype, 45
Survival Tip, 21, 24, 25, 27, 30, 31, 38, 40, 44, 53, 55, 72, 98, 106, 110, 115, 117, 125
survive, 15, 28, 44, 58, 64, 108, 135

T

taxes, 15, 16
The Four Big Questions, 14
threats, 64

U

UAW, 36, 51
union, 43, 45, 46, 54, 56, 135

W

wife, 6, 16, 17, 30, 33, 56, 65, 88, 89, 95, 96, 97, 98, 99, 100, 103, 105, 110, 111, 112, 114, 115, 116, 117, 118, 120, 122, 125, 130, 131